WANDA E. BRUNSTETTER'S

Amish Friends
COMFORT FOODS
COOKBOOK

More Than 270 Recipes that Taste like Home and Love

BARBOUR
PUBLISHING

© 2024 by Wanda E. Brunstetter

Print ISBN 978-1-63609-973-6

All rights reserved. No part of this publication may be reproduced or transmitted for commercial purposes, except for brief quotations in printed reviews, without written permission of the publisher. Reproduced text may not be used on the World Wide Web. No Barbour Publishing content may be used as artificial intelligence training data for machine learning, or in any similar software development.

Scripture taken from the New King James Version®. Copyright © 1982 by Thomas Nelson, Inc. Used by permission. All rights reserved.

Cover Photograph (top): © Doyle Yoder Photography

Published by Barbour Publishing, Inc., 1810 Barbour Drive, Uhrichsville, Ohio 44683, www.barbourbooks.com

Our mission is to inspire the world with the life-changing message of the Bible.

Member of the
Evangelical Christian
Publishers Association

Printed in China.

INTRODUCTION

There seems to be a lot of talk about comfort foods these days. Maybe that's because we all feel the need to be soothed, especially during times of stress.

Why do we turn to food when our emotions are on a roller coaster? Why do certain foods bring us comfort? While this new cookbook won't answer the psychological questions, it will provide you with recipes for a variety of comfort foods that could help you through a bad day or add joy to a special occasion. Although food can't make a person's problems or feelings go away, it can make us feel better mentally and physically, if only for a little while.

Foods that are considered comforting are based on individual preference. Some of us crave sweets, while others prefer high-carb meals or the enjoyment of eating healthy treats. Basically, most any food could be considered as a comfort food if it's something that brings you pleasure and enjoyment.

Comfort foods can trigger our brain's reward system and pleasure centers, leading to the production of dopamine. This can boost a person's mood or even make them feel so relaxed that they might fall asleep.

Some of my favorite comfort foods are creamy tomato soup, chocolate brownies, cottage cheese with pineapple slices, homemade vanilla ice cream, and toasted cheese sandwiches. I also enjoy drinking comforting beverages such as warm apple cider, maple-flavored herbal tea, and guava juice over ice.

Inside this new comfort food cookbook, you will find over two hundred recipes for delicious heartwarming foods, divided into traditional categories from main dishes and sides to desserts and snacks.

I wish to thank my editor, Rebecca Germany, for compiling the recipes submitted by Amish and Mennonite friends who live in plain communities around the country.

Wanda E. Brunstetter

Therefore, whether you eat or drink,
or whatever you do, do all to the glory of God.
1 CORINTHIANS 10:31

Blessed be the God and Father of our
Lord Jesus Christ, the Father of mercies
and God of all comfort, who comforts
us in all our tribulation, that we may
be able to comfort those who are in any
trouble, with the comfort with which
we ourselves are comforted by God.

2 Corinthians 1:3–4

TABLE OF CONTENTS

PRECIOUS MEMORIES

by Amish friend LYDIANN YODER, Andover, OH

Reprinted from *Wanda E. Brunstetter's*
Amish Friends Gatherings Cookbook

My dad's family made many cherished memories by celebrating family members' birthdays. These were always evenings we looked forward to and were enjoyed by all.

My dad's birthday was in March. We would not tell him which evening everyone was coming so he'd be surprised. But his family's special efforts in cleaning up the house would always make him suspicious. The relatives would arrive with their families and freezers of homemade ice cream with toppings. A beautifully decorated cake made by Uncle Lester's wife would be admired by all. The cakes were made in various shapes and designs.

Soon the evening was over and the ice cream eaten. But we could look forward to Grandpa's birthday in June. Strawberries would be ripe by then and included in the menu. My uncles would tease me because I never wanted my strawberries on top of my ice cream but in a separate bowl.

Grandmother, two uncles, and two aunts had birthdays in September. They were all celebrated the same evening, usually at my grandparents' house. Again came the many freezers of ice cream with ice put in a gunnysack and chopped up. The iceman would bring ice twice a week.

Our uncle who lived closer to town would sometimes bring store-bought ice cream. We always chose the homemade first, though. Since no strawberries were in season then and we had no freezers to keep any, we'd have chocolate dip to put on our ice cream instead. It was so yummy, especially when it was still warm and poured over the ice cream. I have included the recipe (page 207).

Time has a way of slipping by. We are now making memories for our families. Let's not be too busy to make family members' birthdays special by sharing it with them.

MEMORABLE BEVERAGES

If it weren't for hot water,
the teakettle wouldn't sing.

AMISH SAYING

ICED TEA

2 quarts water
12 sprigs mint
4 tea bags

1 cup lemon juice
2 cups sugar

In a saucepan, heat water and brew mint and tea for 1 hour. Add lemon juice and sugar. Put into jars and seal. To 1 quart concentrate, add 2 quarts water and ice to make 1 gallon. Adjust to taste. You can use more mint and no tea bags if desired.

MIRIAM BYLER, Spartansburg, PA

Sun Tea

10 Lipton tea bags
1⅓ cups sugar
1 envelope lemonade mix

On a sunny day, put tea bags in glass gallon jar and fill with water. Set in sun for 3 hours. Remove tea bags and add sugar, lemonade mix, and more water if needed to fill the gallon. Chill.

Malinda Gingerich, Spartansburg, PA

Good Lemonade

1 cup sugar
1 cup lemon juice

9 cups cold water

Combine sugar and juice, stirring until sugar is dissolved. Add water.

Emma Zook, Navarre, OH

Quick Root Beer

2 cups sugar
1 gallon warm water

4 teaspoons root beer extract
1 teaspoon yeast

Dissolve sugar in some of the warm water, stirring. Add remaining water, extract, and yeast. Set in sun for 4 hours or until ready. Chill.

Emma Beiler, Delta, PA

Homemade Hot Chocolate Mix

*This recipe was shared by a friend along with the
mix for Christmas one year. It is very rich and sweet.
Perfect for comfort on a cloudy winter day.*

3 cups dry nonfat or
whole milk powder
2 cups powdered sugar

1½ cups cocoa powder
¼ teaspoon salt

Whisk together all ingredients in large bowl or place ingredients in a food processor, pulsing until chocolate is finely ground. Store in an airtight container.

To make a cup:

Mix ⅓ cup mixture into 1 cup hot milk. Top with whipped cream, miniature marshmallows, or other desired topping.

Salome Beiler, Woodward, PA

Yummy Hot Chocolate

This is delicious!

¼ cup brown sugar
2 tablespoons cocoa powder
⅛ teaspoon salt
¼ cup hot water

1 tablespoon butter
4 cups milk
1 teaspoon vanilla
12 large marshmallows

In a large saucepan, combine sugar, cocoa, and salt. Stir in hot water and butter. Bring to a boil. Add milk, vanilla, and marshmallows. Heat until hot, remove from heat, and let marshmallows melt for about 10 minutes. Stir and serve.

Kari Petersheim, Fredericktown, OH

CAPPUCCINO MIX

Delicious for those days when the snow is flying outside your window.

2 cups dry milk
⅔ cup french vanilla creamer
1 cup powdered coffee creamer
¼ teaspoon salt

⅔ cup chocolate milk mix
¼ cup coconut sugar
  or cane sugar
¼ heaping cup instant coffee

Mix all ingredients and store in an airtight container. Add ¼ cup mixture to 1 cup hot water and mix until dissolved. Adjust mixture-to-water ratio to your taste.

NELSON AND JOANN MILLER FAMILY, Fredericktown, OH

Pumpkin Spice Latte

2 cups milk
4 teaspoons pumpkin puree
4 teaspoons maple syrup
1 teaspoon cinnamon

½ cup strong brewed coffee
Whipped cream
Nutmeg

In a saucepan, combine milk, pumpkin, maple syrup, and cinnamon and bring to a boil, whisking vigorously until mixture is foamy. Divide coffee into 2 mugs and divide milk mixture on top. Add a dollop of whipped cream and a sprinkle of nutmeg on top.

Note: in place of maple syrup you can use 3 tablespoons brown sugar plus 1 tablespoon water.

Mrs. Melvin Schlabach, Dayton, PA

ICED HONEY MOCHA

Ice
1 cup cold brewed coffee
3 to 5 teaspoons honey
½ tablespoon cocoa powder

3 to 4 tablespoons half-
and-half, coconut milk,
or almond milk

Fill a wide-mouth pint-size mason jar halfway full with ice. Top with coffee, honey, and cocoa powder. Screw lid on mason jar and shake vigorously until cocoa powder is well mixed into the drink. Top with half-and-half. Mix until blended.

KATHY NISLEY, Loudonville, OH

EGGNOG

2 eggs
¼ cup maple syrup
4 cups milk
¼ teaspoon salt

1 teaspoon vanilla
½ teaspoon nutmeg
½ teaspoon cinnamon

Mix all ingredients together in a blender. Serve. Makes 1 quart.

KARI PETERSHEIM, Fredericktown, OH

FAVORITE EGGNOG

We use this quite often as a healthy drink.
Delicious and a good source of protein.

3 eggs
1 teaspoon vanilla
½ teaspoon cinnamon

¼ cup sugar
Milk

Beat eggs thoroughly. Add vanilla, cinnamon, and sugar. Beat well. Pour into a quart jar or pitcher and fill with cold milk.

MRS. MELVIN SCHLABACH, Dayton, PA

Jamocha Shake

1 cup cold brewed coffee
1 cup milk
3 tablespoons sugar
3 cups vanilla ice cream
3 tablespoons chocolate syrup

In a blender, place coffee, milk, and sugar, blending on medium speed for 15 seconds to dissolve sugar. Add ice cream and chocolate syrup and blend until smooth and creamy.

Doretta Mast, LaGrange, IN

Pumpkin Cheesecake Shake

1 cup crushed ice
⅓ cup milk
¼ cup cottage cheese
1 to 2 ounces cream cheese
   or 2 tablespoons heavy
   whipping cream
2 tablespoons pumpkin puree
¼ teaspoon pumpkin pie spice
Dash vanilla
Dash salt
⅛ teaspoon xanthan gum
3 smidgens stevia
½ scoop whey protein
   powder (optional)

Put all ingredients in a blender and blend until smooth.

Ranae Yoder, Kalona, IA

Strawberry Milkshake

1 quart frozen strawberries
½ cup sugar
5 cups milk

Put all ingredients in a blender and blend until smooth. Delicious to enjoy on a warm summer day.

Marlene Stoltzfus, Gap, PA

SLUSHY DRINK

1 (6 ounce) package
   gelatin of any flavor
1 cup sugar
2 cups boiling water

46 ounces pineapple juice
1 quart cold water
Lemon-lime soda

Mix together gelatin, sugar, and boiling water, stirring until all is dissolved. Mix in pineapple juice and cold water. Freeze. Thaw a little and serve with lemon-lime soda.

ELLA SHETLER, West Salem, OH

RHUBARB FRUIT SLUSH

½ steamer full of
   chopped rhubarb
12 ounces frozen lemonade
16 ounces frozen orange juice
6 cups sugar

3½ quarts water
2 packages tropical punch
   Kool-Aid mix
Lemon-lime soda

Place rhubarb in steamer with water and steam. To a kettle, add lemonade, orange juice, sugar, 3½ quarts water, and Kool-Aid. Heat to melt sugar. Strain rhubarb and add juice to mixture. Cool and pour into containers to freeze. To serve, thaw slightly and pour lemon-lime soda over.

GLENDA SCHWARTZ, Milford, IN

RHUBARB JUICE

4 pounds rhubarb, chopped
4 quarts water
2 cups sugar

1 cup orange juice
1 cup pineapple juice

In a saucepan, combine rhubarb and water and cook until softened. Drain and add sugar, orange juice, and pineapple juice to rhubarb juice. Cold pack in quart jars for 5 minutes to seal. Serve juice over ice and add cold water to adjust taste for a refreshing drink.

MIRIAM BYLER, Spartansburg, PA

Canned Cider

In a large pot, heat apple cider to at least 180 degrees. Hold at that temperature for 10 minutes. Ladle into hot quart canning jars. Screw on 2-part lids and turn jars down. When completely cool, lids should be sealed.

This tastes like fresh cider for a great drink during winter, but don't drink too much. If unwell with flu, drink with pineapple juice. It is especially good for children when they are sick. It chases away the cold or flu quicker and is a treat for sick children.

Mrs. Reuben (Anna) Lapp, Rockville, IN

Stomach Comfort Drinks

- When feeling unwell, heat milk and soak saltine crackers or toasted bread in it to eat. Season with salt and pepper as desired. It is light on an upset stomach.
- Gelatin water or thickened gelatin is supposed to ease an upset stomach. Cherry flavor tastes the best, most satisfying.

Emma Gingerich, Bremen, OH

Golden Milk Tonic

4 cups milk
3 teaspoons turmeric
2 teaspoons cinnamon
2 teaspoons ginger
¼ teaspoon pepper
2 tablespoons maple syrup or honey

Blend all ingredients in a blender or bring to a simmer in a saucepan while whisking well. Store in the refrigerator and add some to your coffee each day. Curcumin (active ingredient in turmeric) is great for arthritis, and you need the black pepper to help absorb it. Also, this tonic is great for skin health, depression, digestion, immunity, anti-inflammation, and higher antioxidant and iron levels.

Miriam Byler, Spartansburg, PA

Memories
of My Grandma

Mary Miller, Junction City, OH

A memory I have of my grandma when I was young was to drink the sweet cherry juice that Grandma drained off her canned cherries. She always put it in a green glass, which was so special to us young ones. Eventually, those two green glasses disappeared off her sink shelf and got replaced with clear glasses, which my younger cousins made memories with their juice at Grandma's house. I often wondered what happened to those two green glasses. When they had the estate sale after Grandpa and Grandma passed away, I saw those glasses again. I realized then that other grandchildren had also wondered what had happened to those glasses, while other grandchildren treasured the clear ones. Each holds special memories of sharing juice with Grandma.

Canned Cherries or Berries

8 pounds fresh cherries or whole berries (approximately)
Sugar
Water

Wash and pit cherries, discarding any bruised or moldy fruit. For sweet cherries, use a light syrup of 1 cup sugar to 6 cups water. For more tart cherries, use a medium syrup of 2 cups sugar to 5 cups water. In a saucepan, dissolve sugar in water, simmering about 5 minutes until clear. Fill 4 hot, sterile quart jars with about ½ cup syrup each. Fill jars with cherries, shaking them to evenly distribute and inserting a knife to release any air pockets. Top with syrup, leaving an inch of head space. Wipe jar rims and place 2-part lids finger tight. Seal jars covered in hot water bath for 30 minutes.

Nostalgic Breakfast Foods

Contentment comes not from great wealth but from few wants.

AMISH SAYING

Yogurt Parfait

2½ cups granola
8 ounces cream cheese, softened
½ cup sour cream
4 cups yogurt

2 tablespoons lemon juice
8 ounces whipped topping
Fruit, sliced or chopped

Spread granola in bottom of a 9x13-inch pan. In a bowl, blend cream cheese, sour cream, yogurt, and lemon juice. Fold in whipped topping. Spread over granola. Top with fruit.

Miriam Coblentz, Greenfield, OH

Thermos Oatmeal

2 cups oats
2 tablespoons brown sugar
1 teaspoon cinnamon
½ teaspoon nutmeg
1½ cups water or milk

½ teaspoon vanilla
2 tablespoons maple syrup
½ cup chopped nuts,
   shredded coconut, and/
   or chocolate chips

In a thermos, mix oats, brown sugar, cinnamon, and nutmeg. Heat water or milk until almost boiling; mix into oats along with vanilla and maple syrup. Stir. Wait a few minutes for oatmeal to thicken. Stir once more then top with your choice of nuts, coconut, and/or chocolate chips. Seal thermos until ready to eat.

Kari Petersheim, Fredericktown, OH

Baked Oatmeal

3 cups oats
2 teaspoons baking powder
1 teaspoon salt
1 cup milk
½ cup melted butter
1 cup brown sugar

2 eggs
2 teaspoons vanilla
Optional additions:
   raisins, chopped nuts,
   chopped apples, etc.

Mix together oats, baking powder, salt, milk, and melted butter. Stir in brown sugar, eggs, and vanilla. Stir in optional additions. Place in a 9x9-inch pan and bake at 350 degrees for 30 minutes. Serve warm with milk or maple syrup.

Malinda Gingerich, Spartansburg, PA

We like to serve this with yogurt and fruit.
Ella Shetler, West Salem, OH

Simply Eggs

Melt butter in a large skillet. Add about 3 tablespoons water. Crack the number of eggs you wish into skillet and sprinkle with salt and pepper. Put lid on the skillet and turn to lowest heat. For a dozen eggs, check after 20 minutes. They are soft and tasty if cooked until just done. Overcooked eggs are rubbery. When eggs are done, pinch a bread bag tie between the lid and skillet to keep the lid from sealing. These eggs are a lot like poached eggs. The handy thing about this recipe is that there is no need to flip the eggs. I have flipped them, and this method keeps them from being dried out.

Jerry and Ida Petersheim, Kenton, OH

Omelets

Fillings of choice: fried sausage, fried bacon, cooked potatoes, chopped ham, onion, green pepper, mushrooms, etc.

2 eggs, beaten
Salt and pepper to taste
Cheese, sliced

Prepare your fillings. If desired, fry onion, green pepper, and mushrooms with sausage. In a bowl, beat eggs and season to taste. Put butter in an omelet pan or skillet and pour egg in. Cook over low heat until egg begins to set. Lift edges with spatula to let unset egg run underneath. Cook a little longer, then flip the egg and immediately lay cheese on top. Spread filling on half of omelet. Fold other half over top filled portion. Carefully slide out onto a warmed plate. If needed, keep omelet warm in a 150-degree oven until ready to serve.

Ida Bontrager, Kenton, OH

Egg Muffins

12 eggs
½ cup milk
½ teaspoon salt
½ teaspoon pepper

1 to 2 cups meat of choice
(ham, bacon, sausage),
cooked and crumbled
½ cup diced peppers
½ cup diced onion
½ cup additional chopped
vegetables of choice (optional)

In a bowl, beat eggs and milk together. Add salt and pepper. Stir in meat, peppers, onion, and vegetables. Spray or grease muffin tins. Divide egg mixture into 12 muffin holes almost to the top. Bake at 325 degrees for 20 minutes or until tops are firm. Cool slightly before serving.

Elizabeth Esh, Paradise, PA

Corn Mush

I remember this as a delicious breakfast on winter mornings.
We ate it with maple syrup or apple butter.

6 cups water
3 cups cornmeal

2 teaspoons salt
2 cups milk

Bring water to boil in a large pot. Mix cornmeal, salt, and milk and add to boiling water. Stir constantly until it starts boiling again. Cover and turn heat to low for 20 minutes. Divide into 2 greased loaf pans. Let stand overnight. The next morning, slice and fry.

Mrs. Melvin Schlabach, Dayton, PA

Cornmeal Mush

When at home with my parents, we ate lots of mush for breakfast with eggs. We put ketchup and molasses on the fried mush. Today we only use ketchup. Eating this brings special memories of sitting at the table with my parents and family. My parents were both ninety-three years old when they died three years apart.

3 quarts water
2 teaspoons salt
3½ cups cornmeal

¼ cup flour
3 cups water

In a large kettle, bring 3 quarts water to boil. In a bowl, mix salt, cornmeal, and flour. Add 3 cups water and mix until all is wet. Add to boiling water and cook for 1 hour over low heat. Just keep it bubbling. You can eat it hot or prepare it for frying later: Put mush in a 9x13-inch pan and refrigerate several hours. Slice and fry.

Sadie Fisher, Aaronsburg, PA

Breakfast Haystack

Biscuits or toast
Fried potatoes
Scrambled eggs
Sausage or chopped
   ham, cooked

Tomatoes, diced
Onions, chopped
Peppers, chopped
Shredded cheese
Cheese sauce

Layer prepared ingredients on your plate in order given or adjust to your taste. Enjoy!

Melvin D. Schlabach, Dayton, PA

Quick and Easy Breakfast Casserole

Biscuit dough or hash browns
1 pound sausage
¾ cup diced green peppers
½ cup diced onion
1 small can sliced mushrooms

10 eggs, scrambled
½ to 1 package Little
  Smokies sausages
Cheese sauce
Bacon, fried and crumbled

Put biscuit dough or hash browns into bottom of casserole dish and bake at 350 degrees for 10 to 15 minutes. Fry sausage with green peppers and onions. Add mushrooms and put on top of biscuit. Top with scrambled eggs and Little Smokies. Cover with your favorite cheese sauce. Sprinkle with bacon and bake for 15 minutes.

Emma Esh, Gordonville, PA

Breakfast Burrito Casserole

1 can cream of mushroom soup
1½ cups sour cream
½ cup salsa or taco sauce
4 large tortillas, cut into pieces

1 pound sausage, fried
8 eggs, scrambled
2 cups shredded cheddar cheese

In a bowl, mix mushroom soup, sour cream, and salsa. Spread half of mixture in a 9x13-inch pan. Layer on tortilla pieces, sausage, scrambled egg, and half of the cheese. Spread remaining sauce on top then top with remaining cheese. Bake at 350 degrees for 45 to 50 minutes.

Mrs. Roman (Alma) Yoder, Patriot, OH

Potato and Sausage Casserole

5 pounds sausage
2 tablespoons seasoned salt
2 tablespoons onion powder
1 tablespoon taco seasoning
5 pounds potatoes
2 cups milk

1 pound Velveeta
  cheese, shredded
1 (8 ounce) package
  cream cheese
½ cup butter
1 (16 ounce) tub sour cream

In a large skillet, season sausage with seasoned salt, onion powder, and taco seasoning; fry until browned. Drain grease. Shred potatoes and either steam in water (then drain) or fry until tender. Mix potatoes, sausage, and milk into a large roasting pan. In a saucepan, mix Velveeta cheese, cream cheese, butter, and sour cream and melt over low heat. Pour over potato mixture. Bake at 350 degrees for 45 minutes until hot and bubbly to your liking.

IDA BONTRAGER, Kenton, OH

Sausage Gravy

½ pound sausage

4 to 5 tablespoons flour

4 tablespoons butter

½ teaspoon salt

¼ teaspoon pepper

4½ cups milk

In a large skillet, fry sausage until no longer pink and drain grease if necessary. Stir in flour, butter, salt, and pepper. Stir over heat until butter is melted. Gradually add milk, stirring constantly. Bring to a boil; boil and stir for 2 minutes until thickened. This recipe is easy to adjust to your liking: if you'd rather have it thicker, add more flour; and if you'd rather have it thinner, add more milk. Serve over warm biscuits.

Malinda Gingerich, Spartansburg, PA

Delicious Pancakes

1¼ cups flour
1 teaspoon sugar
¾ teaspoon salt
1½ tablespoons baking powder

2 eggs
⅓ cup butter or
    margarine, melted
1 cup milk

In a bowl, sift together flour, sugar, salt, and baking powder. In another bowl, beat eggs slightly. Add butter and milk. Mix in sifted mixture. Beat only until all flour is mixed in. Bake batter on a lightly greased hot griddle until both sides are lightly browned.

Anita Petersheim, Fredericktown, OH

Dutch Baby

1 stick butter
8 eggs
2 cups flour
2 cups milk

1 teaspoon salt
1 teaspoon baking powder
1 teaspoon vanilla

Cut butter into a 9x13-inch pan. Melt in oven at 400 degrees. In a blender or bowl with mixer, blend eggs, flour, milk, salt, baking powder, and vanilla. Pour over melted butter. Bake until puffy, 20 to 25 minutes. When done, sprinkle with powdered sugar and serve warm with maple syrup.

Anita Petersheim, Fredericktown, OH

PANCAKE PIZZA

3 cups pancake batter
12 eggs, scrambled
1 cup shredded cheese
6 cups white sausage gravy

1 pound bacon, fried
  and crumbled
Maple syrup

Pour batter into a greased 9x13-inch pan. Bake at 350 degrees for 10 to 15 minutes until done. Remove from oven. Layer on scrambled eggs and cheese. Pour gravy on top. Sprinkle with bacon. Serve with maple syrup.

JERRY AND MARY HERTZLER, Charlotte Hall, MD

WAFFLES

2 cups flour
4 teaspoons baking powder
½ teaspoon salt

2 eggs, separated
1¾ cups milk
4 tablespoons butter, melted

Sift flour, baking powder, and salt into a mixing bowl. Add beaten egg yolks and milk. Beat thoroughly. Add butter and beaten egg whites. Fry in waffle iron on medium heat.

ELI AND ELSIE MILLER, Thurman, OH

Peaches and Cream Waffles

Waffles:

2¼ cups flour
1½ cups quick oats
1½ tablespoons baking powder
¾ teaspoon cinnamon
¾ teaspoon salt

3 eggs, slightly beaten
2¼ cups milk
9 tablespoons butter, melted
3 tablespoons brown sugar

In a bowl, stir together flour, oats, baking powder, cinnamon, and salt. In another bowl, mix eggs, milk, butter, and brown sugar. Add dry mixture and blend until moist. Bake batter in waffle iron until lightly browned.

Cream:

8 ounces cream cheese
¼ cup powdered sugar

2 cups whipped topping

In a bowl, beat cream cheese and powdered sugar. Fold in whipped topping.

Filling:

3 cups water
⅓ cup clear jel
½ cup sugar

¼ cup peach gelatin mix
1 quart canned or fresh
   ripe peaches, drained

In a saucepan, combine water, clear jel, and sugar. Heat until thickened. Add gelatin and peaches.

To serve: Spread cream onto waffles and top with peach filling.

Kari Petersheim, Fredericktown, OH

Caramelized Nutty French Toast

1 cup brown sugar
½ cup butter
¼ cup maple syrup
1 loaf bread, sliced into
    about 12 pieces

Cream cheese
Cinnamon
6 eggs
2 cups milk
1 teaspoon vanilla

Generously grease a 9x13-inch pan. In a saucepan, combine sugar, butter, and maple syrup and cook until sugar is dissolved. Put in bottom of baking pan. Spread 6 slices bread with cream cheese and sprinkle with cinnamon. Place in a single layer in pan with cream cheese facing up. Top with the other 6 slices bread. In a bowl, beat together eggs, milk, and vanilla and pour over bread. Cover and let set in refrigerator overnight. In the morning, prepare nut topping and spread on top of bread. Bake at 350 degrees for 50 minutes or until puffy and golden brown. If top browns too fast, cover with foil until done.

Nut Topping:

3 tablespoons corn syrup
1½ cups chopped nuts

½ cup melted butter
½ cup brown sugar

In a bowl, combine all ingredients until well mixed.

MALINDA GINGERICH, Spartansburg, PA

Raspberry-Stuffed French Toast

2 slices bread
Raspberry pie filling or jam
Cream cheese, softened

Egg
Milk
Oil

Spread cream cheese on a slice of bread and raspberry pie filling on the other. Sandwich together. In a bowl, beat together egg and milk. Dip sandwich into mixture until fully moistened. Fry in hot oil until browned on both sides. Eat with whipped cream.

ELI AND ELSIE MILLER, Thurman, OH

OVERNIGHT DANISH

1 cup butter
5 cups flour
½ teaspoon salt
1 tablespoon yeast
¼ cup warm water

3 eggs, beaten
¾ cup warm water
½ cup sugar
Pie filling

Cut butter into flour and salt until it looks like cornmeal. Dissolve yeast in ¼ cup warm water. Add eggs, yeast, and ¾ cup warm water to flour. Mix in sugar. Refrigerate dough 6 hours or overnight.

CREAM CHEESE FILLING:

2 (8 ounce) packages cream cheese, softened
½ cup sugar
6 tablespoons flour

2 tablespoons lemon juice
2 egg yolks
1 teaspoon grated lemon peel

Mix all together until smooth. Roll dough out into a rectangle, spread cream cheese filling down the middle third, and top with pie filling. Slice uncovered dough on both sides into 1-inch strips (I use a pizza cutter). Fold dough slices over middle in a back-and-forth braiding fashion. Let rise. Bake at 375 degrees for approximately 20 minutes until browned. When cooled, frost.

FROSTING:

1 cup powdered sugar
2 tablespoons milk

2 tablespoons melted butter
½ teaspoon maple flavoring

Mix all ingredients together until smooth. If it needs to be thinner to spread, add a splash of milk.

MALINDA GINGERICH, Spartansburg, PA

COZY AND CRUSTY BREADS

*May love of parents, deep and true, and
sweet familiar ways always be remembered
and stay always close to you.*

AMISH SAYING

CORN BREAD FOR SERVING WITH BEANS

This was a childhood favorite that I still crave and make for supper.

¾ cup butter
1 cup sugar
3 eggs
1¾ cups flour

1 cup cornmeal
4½ teaspoons baking powder
1 teaspoon salt
1⅔ cups milk

In a mixing bowl, cream butter, sugar, and eggs. In another bowl, combine flour, cornmeal, baking powder, and salt. Alternate adding dry mixture and milk to creamed mixture. Pour into a greased 9x13-inch pan. Bake at 400 degrees for 22 to 27 minutes. Serve hot corn bread with hot navy beans and milk for a delicious and filling supper.

MARY MILLER, Junction City, OH

CORN BREAD WITH HOT HONEY BUTTER

1 cup cornmeal
2 teaspoons sugar
¾ cup flour
1 tablespoon baking powder
1 teaspoon salt

½ teaspoon baking soda
6 tablespoons unsalted
  butter, melted
1½ cups buttermilk
2 large eggs

In a large bowl, mix cornmeal, sugar, flour, baking powder, salt, and baking soda. In another bowl, add melted butter and whisk in buttermilk and eggs. Pour wet mixture into dry mixture, mixing until well incorporated. Pour into a greased 9x9-inch pan and bake at 425 degrees for 20 to 25 minutes.

HOT HONEY BUTTER:

1 stick salted butter, softened
3 tablespoons honey

½ teaspoon hot sauce

In a small bowl, mix all ingredients together. Taste for spice level and add more hot sauce if desired. Serve with warm corn bread. Butter can be kept at room temperature for 2 days. It can be added to other dishes like roasted carrots or grilled corn on the cob.

ESTHER L. MILLER, Fredericktown, OH

ANGEL BISCUITS

6 cups flour
3 teaspoons baking powder
1½ teaspoons salt
1 teaspoon baking soda
¼ cup sugar

1 cup shortening
¼ cup warm water
1 tablespoon yeast
2 cups sour milk or buttermilk

In a bowl, mix flour, baking powder, salt, baking soda, and sugar. Cut in shortening. In a small bowl, dissolve yeast in warm water. Add milk. Mix into dry ingredients until just combined. Roll dough out on a floured surface and cut with biscuit cutter. Let rise on an ungreased baking sheet for 25 to 40 minutes. Bake at 400 degrees for 12 to 15 minutes.

ESTHER L. MILLER, Fredericktown, OH

GARLIC CHEDDAR BISCUITS

1 cup flour
1 tablespoon sugar
2 teaspoons baking powder
½ tablespoon garlic salt or
    powder, or use fresh ground
    garlic from your garden

¼ teaspoon salt (or 1 tablespoon
    if using garlic powder
    rather than garlic salt)
¼ cup cold butter
1 cup grated cheddar cheese
½ cup milk

Mix all dry ingredients; add butter, cheese, and milk. Form biscuits. Bake at 400 degrees for 8 to 10 minutes.

MRS. REUBEN LAPP, Marshall, IN

Homemade Crescent Roll Crust

½ cup butter, chilled
1 tablespoon yeast
¼ cup warm water
1 egg

¼ cup milk, scalded
2 cups flour
¼ cup sugar
½ teaspoon salt

Melt chilled butter, then cool again until set. This will make your crust flaky. In a bowl, dissolve yeast in warm water; add egg and scalded milk. In another bowl, mix flour, sugar, and salt. Mix in butter. Stir mixture into yeast just until combined and sticking together. Do not overmix. Press onto a large cookie sheet and let rise. Bake at 350 degrees for approximately 15 minutes until firm. Makes a good base for breakfast, vegetable, or fruit pizza.

Malinda Gingerich, Spartansburg, PA

Mom's Dinner Rolls

2 cups very warm water
  (potato water works best)
2 tablespoons yeast
1 egg, warmed
2 teaspoons salt
⅓ cup sugar
¼ cup oil
1 cup bread flour
5 to 7 cups all-purpose
  flour, divided

Dissolve yeast in warm water. Add warmed egg, salt, sugar, oil, bread flour, and 1 cup all-purpose flour. Beat 150 times with slotted spoon. Add remaining flour. Grease top of dough and cover. Let rise about 45 minutes. Punch down dough then let rise again for about 30 minutes. Separate dough into about 36 rolls. Place on a baking sheet and grease tops. Let rise 1 to 1½ hours. Bake at 400 degrees for 15 minutes.

Pepperoni and Cheese Rolls Variation:

Use above recipe and put 2 slices pepperoni and some mozzarella cheese inside each roll and form the dough around it into a ball. Bake.

Malinda Gingerich, Spartansburg, PA

Potato Buns

2 cups warm water
2 tablespoons yeast
1 cup sugar
1 tablespoon salt
1 cup shortening
5 eggs
2 cups mashed potatoes
10 cups flour

In a large mixing bowl, dissolve yeast in warm water then add sugar, salt, shortening, and eggs. Mix in potatoes. Lastly, add flour and mix well. Let rise to double size. Punch down dough and let rise again. Roll out and cut into individual buns. Place on a baking sheet and let rise. Bake at 375 degrees for 20 minutes.

Mrs. Daniel Stoltzfus, Nottingham, PA

OUR FAVORITE BREAD

½ cup sugar
4 teaspoons salt
2 teaspoons lecithin
1 tablespoon shortening

4 cups warm water (110 degrees)
3 tablespoons yeast
⅓ cup oil
10 cups flour

In a mixing bowl, blend sugar, salt, lecithin, and shortening. Add warm water, yeast, and oil. Immediately stir in flour until able to knead. Add more flour until properly stiff. Cover lightly and let rise. Knead every 15 minutes for 1 hour. Divide into 4 greased loaf pans. Use fork to poke holes in top of loaf. Let rise 45 minutes. Bake at 350 degrees for 30 minutes.

MRS. LYDIA D. SHETLER, Sugar Grove, PA

GRANDMA'S HONEY WHEAT BREAD

4 cups warm water
2 heaping tablespoons yeast
1 egg
¾ cup oil
½ cup honey

½ cup wheat germ
1 tablespoon salt
2 cups whole-wheat flour
9 cups all-purpose flour
  (approximately)

Preheat oven to 350 degrees. Whisk together first 7 ingredients. Add wheat flour first and up to 9 cups all-purpose flour. Let rise until double. Punch down and shape into loaves. Let rise to double again. Bake for 50 to 60 minutes. Yields 4 large loaves or 5 small loaves.

EMMA RABER, Holmesville, OH

CINNAMON BUTTER

1 cup butter, softened
½ cup powdered sugar

¼ cup honey
2 teaspoons cinnamon

Whisk all ingredients together until smooth. Delicious with warm home-made bread.

MARLENE STOLTZFUS, Gap, PA

Amish Peanut Butter Spread

2 cups brown sugar
1 cup water
1 teaspoon maple extract

2 cups peanut butter
1 (16 ounce) jar
marshmallow crème

In a saucepan, combine brown sugar, water, and maple extract and bring to a boil. Blend peanut butter and marshmallow crème. Then blend both mixtures together until smooth. Serve as a spread on bread or crackers.

Saloma Stutzman, Navarre, OH

FRENCH HERB BREAD

3 tablespoons yeast
3 cups warm water
3 tablespoons sugar
6 tablespoons olive oil
1 tablespoon salt
1 teaspoon oregano

3 tablespoons minced onion or
  1 teaspoon onion powder
3 tablespoons parsley flakes
1 teaspoon garlic powder
7 to 7½ cups flour

In a large mixing bowl, mix yeast, water, and sugar. Allow to dissolve. Add oil, salt, oregano, onion, parsley, and garlic powder. Work in flour until it forms a dough that can be handled. Cover and let rise to double. Turn dough out onto floured counter and shape into 2 french loaves. Let rise until tripled. Bake at 350 degrees for 25 minutes. When cooled, slice in 1-inch pieces and spread with butter between slices. Delicious served with soup. You can also put the bread in the freezer to use later. Reheat at 400 degrees for 15 minutes.

NELSON AND JOANN MILLER FAMILY, Fredericktown, OH

Garlic Loaf

2 cans refrigerated biscuits
3 tablespoons butter, divided
2 cloves garlic, minced

3 tablespoons grated
Parmesan cheese

Melt 1 tablespoon butter and pour in bottom of a loaf pan. Lay 1 log of biscuits on each side of the pan. Fan out biscuits and drizzle remaining butter melted with garlic over the top, in between, and around the sides. Scatter cheese over top and in between biscuits. Bake at 350 degrees for 30 minutes, or until center is solid. Serve warm, pulling apart the sections.

Pizza Bread

1 tablespoon yeast
1 cup warm water
1 teaspoon sugar
2 tablespoons olive oil
1 teaspoon salt
2½ cups flour
2 eggs, divided

1 teaspoon Italian
seasoning, divided
1 teaspoon seasoned
salt, divided
4 ounces shaved ham
4 ounces sliced pepperoni
1 cup shredded
mozzarella cheese

In a mixing bowl, dissolve yeast in warm water. Add sugar, oil, salt, and flour, and mix until combined. Cover with cloth and let rise until doubled. Roll out on floured cookie sheet. Beat 1 egg and spread over dough. Sprinkle with ½ teaspoon Italian seasoning and ½ teaspoon seasoned salt. Put slices of ham and pepperoni in center of dough and spread cheese over all. Fold in sides of pizza, covering meats and cheese. Spread another beaten egg over top, and sprinkle remaining seasonings on top. Bake at 350 degrees for 20 minutes.

Lovina Miller, Shipshewana, IN

PULL BUNS

We used to call this "Monkey Bread."

1 cup milk, scalded
⅓ cup sugar
⅓ cup melted butter
½ teaspoon salt
1 tablespoon yeast dissolved
    in ¼ cup warm water

3 eggs, well beaten
3¾ cups flour (approximately)
¾ cup sugar
½ cup chopped nuts
3 teaspoons cinnamon
Butter, melted

In a bowl, combine scalded milk, ⅓ cup sugar, ⅓ cup melted butter, and salt. When milk is cooled to lukewarm, add dissolved yeast, eggs, and just enough flour to make a stiff batter. Cover and let rise until mixture doubles. Knead down and let rise again. In a bowl, combine ¾ cup sugar, chopped nuts, and cinnamon. Roll dough into small balls about the size of a whole walnut. Dip into melted butter then roll in sugar-nut mixture. Pile balls loosely in an ungreased angel food cake pan and let rise again for 30 minutes. (Do not use a pan with removable bottom.) Bake at 400 degrees for 10 minutes. Reduce heat to 350 degrees and bake for 30 minutes until browned. Turn pan upside down onto a platter and remove pan immediately. Serve warm. The buns will be stuck together. Everyone just plucks their bun from the mound.

MALINDA GINGERICH, Spartansburg, PA

Black Raspberry Rolls

½ cup sugar
3 tablespoons oil
1½ cups hot water
2 tablespoons yeast
½ cup warm water

2 eggs, beaten
6 cups flour
2 teaspoons salt
1½ cups black raspberry
  pie filling

In a mixing bowl, blend sugar and oil. Add 1½ cups hot water, stirring to cool mixture to lukewarm. Dissolve yeast in ½ cup warm water. When first mixture has cooled, add eggs and yeast. Add flour and salt, beating half of the flour at a time with a mixer. Cover and let rise in refrigerator overnight. The next day, roll dough out into a ½-inch thick rectangle. Spread with pie filling. Roll up and cut into 1-inch slices. Place on greased pans and let rise until doubled in size. Bake at 375 degrees for 15 to 20 minutes, or until slightly browned.

ICING:

1 (8 ounce) package cream
  cheese, softened
½ cup butter, softened

¾ cup marshmallow crème
2 cups powdered sugar

In a bowl, blend cream cheese and butter. Beat in marshmallow crème and powdered sugar until smooth. Spread over warm rolls.

DORETTA MAST, LaGrange, IN

BANANA BREAD

½ cup butter
¾ cup sugar
2 eggs
1 cup mashed banana
¼ cup milk

1 teaspoon vanilla
2 cups flour
1 teaspoon baking soda
1 teaspoon salt
1 cup chopped nuts

In a mixing bowl, blend butter and sugar. Add eggs and banana. Add milk and vanilla. Sift together flour, baking soda, and salt. Mix into wet mixture. Stir in nuts until well incorporated. Pour into 2 well-greased and floured bread pans. Bake at 350 degrees for 60 to 70 minutes.

DELILA SWARTZENTRUBER, West Salem, OH

BANANA SPICE BREAD

1¾ cups sifted flour
2 teaspoons baking powder
¼ teaspoon baking soda
½ teaspoon salt
1 teaspoon cinnamon
¼ teaspoon ground cloves

½ cup honey
2 eggs, well beaten
⅓ cup oil
1 cup mashed banana
½ cup chopped nuts

In a bowl, sift together flour, baking powder, baking soda, salt, cinnamon, and cloves. In another bowl, mix honey, eggs, oil, and banana. Add to dry mixture and beat until smooth. Add nuts. Pour into 2 greased 4½x8½-inch loaf pans. Bake at 350 degrees for 50 to 65 minutes until it tests done. Remove from pans and cool before slicing. You can glaze the loaf if desired.

BETTY MARCAK, Shiner, TX

Pumpkin Cinnamon Rolls

⅔ cup milk
4 tablespoons butter
1 cup pumpkin
4 tablespoons sugar
1 teaspoon salt
2 eggs

2 packages or 2
  tablespoons yeast
4 cups bread flour
2 tablespoons butter, melted
½ cup brown sugar
2 teaspoons cinnamon

In a small saucepan, heat milk and 4 tablespoons butter until warm (110 to 115 degrees). In a large bowl, combine pumpkin, sugar, and salt. Add milk mixture. Beat in eggs and yeast. Add flour and mix well. Cover and let rise until doubled. Turn out raised dough on floured surface and knead until smooth. Roll out into a ½-inch thick rectangle. Brush on melted butter. Mix brown sugar and cinnamon together, and sprinkle over buttered dough. Roll up jelly roll–style starting with long end. Slice into 1-inch slices. Place cut-side down on lightly greased cookie sheet or in round pans with slices almost touching. Let rise in a warm place until doubled. Bake at 350 degrees for 20 minutes. Frost if desired.

MARY ROSE YODER, Shipshewana, IN

Rhubarb Bread

1½ cups brown sugar
⅔ cup oil
1 egg, beaten
1 teaspoon baking soda
1 teaspoon salt
1 teaspoon vanilla

1 cup sour milk
2½ cups flour
1½ cups chopped rhubarb
½ cup chopped nuts
1 tablespoon melted butter
½ cup brown sugar

Mix 1½ cups brown sugar, oil, and egg. Add baking soda, salt, vanilla, and milk. Mix well. Add flour. Mix well. Fold in rhubarb and nuts, mixing until well coated. Pour into 2 greased and floured loaf pans. In a small bowl, combine butter and ½ cup brown sugar. Divide over both loaves batter. Bake at 325 degrees for 1½ hours.

MALINDA GINGERICH, Spartansburg, PA

Zucchini Bread

This was a favorite we would serve at supper with milk.

3 cups flour
2 cups sugar
3 tablespoons cinnamon
1 teaspoon baking soda
¼ teaspoon baking powder

1 teaspoon salt
3 eggs
1 cup oil
1 teaspoon vanilla
2 cups grated zucchini

In a bowl, mix flour, sugar, cinnamon, baking soda, baking powder, and salt. In another bowl, mix eggs, oil, and vanilla. Add dry mixture, stirring well. Add zucchini, mixing until all is combined. Place in a greased 9x13-inch pan. Bake at 350 degrees for 30 to 35 minutes until it tests done.

Mrs. Joseph Miller, Navarre, OH

Healthy Banana Muffins

(Gluten free)

1 egg
¾ cup sugar
⅓ cup applesauce
1 teaspoon vanilla
1⅓ cups mashed banana
1 cup almond flour

½ teaspoon baking soda
2 teaspoons baking powder
1 teaspoon cinnamon
1¼ teaspoons salt
1 cup oats
1 cup chocolate chips

Mix egg, sugar, applesauce, vanilla, and banana. Add flour, baking soda, baking powder, cinnamon, salt, and oatmeal. Stir in chocolate chips. Divide into lined muffin tins. Bake at 350 degrees for 15 to 20 minutes or until lightly browned.

Marlene Stoltzfus, Gap, PA

Cappuccino Muffins

½ cup butter
¾ cup sugar
1 egg
1 teaspoon vanilla
2 cups flour
2½ teaspoons baking powder

1 teaspoon cinnamon
½ teaspoon salt
2 teaspoons instant coffee
1 cup milk
¾ cup mini chocolate chips

In a bowl, blend butter and sugar. Add egg and vanilla. Mix in flour, baking powder, cinnamon, and salt. Dissolve coffee in milk and add to mixture. Stir in chocolate chips. Spoon into lined muffin pan. Bake at 375 degrees for 17 to 20 minutes. Serve with espresso spread.

Espresso Spread:

2 teaspoons instant coffee
2 teaspoons vanilla
8 ounces cream cheese, softened

2 teaspoons sugar
½ cup mini chocolate chips

In a bowl, blend coffee in vanilla to dissolve. Add cream cheese and sugar; mix well. Stir in chocolate chips.

Rosanna Bontrager, Constable, NY

SAVORY SALADS AND SIDES

A garden grows in just a few months, but it takes a long time to grow an old friend.

AMISH SAYING

Strawberry Pretzel Salad

3 tablespoons sugar
¾ cup margarine or butter
2⅔ cups crushed pretzels
1 (8 ounce) package cream
  cheese, softened
1 scant cup sugar

1 cup whipped topping
2 (3 ounce) boxes
  strawberry gelatin
2 cups boiling water
2 quarts frozen strawberries

Cream 3 tablespoons sugar with margarine. Add pretzels. Spread in a 9x13-inch pan and bake at 350 degrees for 10 minutes. Cool. Mix cream cheese, 1 cup sugar, and whipped topping. Pour over cooled crust. Dissolve gelatin in boiling water. Add frozen strawberries. Cool. Pour over cream cheese layer.

Ada Mast, Kalona, IA

BLACKBERRY GELATIN SALAD

3 small boxes black
   raspberry gelatin
3 cups boiling water
2 cups cold water

1 quart blackberry pie filling
1 (8 ounce) package cream
   cheese, softened
1 (8 ounce) tub whipped topping

Dissolve gelatin in boiling water. Add cold water and let set until syrupy. Remove 2 cups liquid and set aside. Add pie filling to remaining gelatin mixture and stir well. Pour into serving dish. Chill until set. Beat cream cheese and slowly add reserved gelatin mixture. Beat well. Fold in whipped topping. Spread over blackberry layer and chill several hours.

ANITA PETERSHEIM, Fredericktown, OH

ORANGE BUTTERMILK SALAD

We served this at our daughter's wedding meal. Very refreshing!

1 (20 ounce) can
   crushed pineapple
1 (6 ounce) package
   orange gelatin

2 cups buttermilk
1 (8 ounce) carton
   whipped topping

In a saucepan, bring pineapple with juice to a boil. Stir in gelatin until dissolved. Remove from heat. Stir in buttermilk. Cool. Add whipped topping. When serving, you can put 1 cherry with 2 mint leaves in the center of each portion.

SALOMIE E. GLICK, Howard, PA

COATED GRAPES

1 cup sour cream
½ cup powdered sugar
1 (8 ounce) package cream
    cheese, softened

1 teaspoon vanilla
Grapes

In a bowl, mix sour cream, powdered sugar, cream cheese, and vanilla until smooth. Add grapes and stir to coat. Chill.

ESTHER J. GINGERICH, Fredericksburg, OH

CRANBERRY SALAD

*No Thanksgiving or Christmas meal is
complete without Mom's cranberry salad.*

1 pound fresh cranberries
3 oranges
2 cups sugar
2 cups crushed, drained
    pineapple

4 (3 ounce) boxes cherry gelatin
7 cups hot water
Optional additions:
    celery, apples, nuts,
    grapes, and the like

Grind cranberries and whole oranges. Add sugar and pineapple. Let stand a few hours to overnight. In a bowl, mix gelatin into hot water, stirring until dissolved. Add cranberry mixture and any preferred additions like diced celery, chopped nuts, and/or cut grapes. Chill until set.

MALINDA GINGERICH, Spartansburg, PA

Broccoli Salad

1 to 2 bunches broccoli
1 head cauliflower
1 pound bacon, fried
  and crumbled
2 cups shredded cheese

1 small onion, diced (optional)
¾ cup sour cream
¾ cup mayonnaise
½ cup sugar
¼ teaspoon salt

In a bowl, chop broccoli and cauliflower; stir in bacon, cheese, and onion. In a small bowl, blend sour cream, mayonnaise, sugar, and salt. Pour over broccoli mixture and stir to coat well. Refrigerate for a few hours before serving.

Eli and Elsie Miller, Thurman, OH

Potato Salad

6 cups shredded potatoes
6 hard-boiled eggs, chopped
¾ cup chopped celery

¾ cup chopped onion
¾ cup chopped green pepper

In a kettle, cook potatoes in a little water until slightly tender. Drain and cool. Add chopped eggs, celery, onion, and green pepper.

Dressing:

1½ cups mayonnaise
2 tablespoons vinegar
1½ tablespoons mustard

1 teaspoon salt
1 cup sugar
¼ cup milk

Mix all ingredients and beat well. Mix into potato mixture, coating well, and chill several hours before serving.

Ella Shetler, West Salem, OH

CORN CHIP SALAD

1 head lettuce, shredded
2 pounds Colby cheese, grated
1 bag corn chips, crushed
2 (15.5 ounce) cans red kidney
beans, drained and rinsed

Combine ingredients. Just before serving, pour dressing over and mix in.

DRESSING:

1 cup Miracle Whip
salad dressing
⅛ cup vinegar
½ teaspoon paprika
2 teaspoons water
¼ cup oil
¾ cup sugar
¼ cup ketchup
1 teaspoon mustard
¼ teaspoon salt

Blend ingredients together.

LAURA MILLER, Mount Vernon, OH

DELICIOUS SALAD

8 large potatoes, peeled,
diced, and cooked
1 box pasta shells, cooked
12 hard-boiled eggs, chopped
2 cups chopped ham
8 ounces Colby cheese, chopped
1 green pepper, chopped
1 medium onion, finely chopped
1 cup pepperoni, chopped
1 cup fried and crumbled bacon
2 tablespoons parsley flakes
1 pint cherry tomatoes

In a large bowl, stir together potatoes, pasta, eggs, ham, cheese, green pepper, onion, pepperoni, bacon, and parsley. Coat with dressing. Gently stir in tomatoes.

DRESSING:

1 quart salad dressing
(e.g., Miracle Whip)
or mayonnaise
1 tablespoon mustard
1 tablespoon vinegar
1 tablespoon salt
1½ cups sugar

Mix all ingredients together until smooth.

MALINDA GINGERICH, Spartansburg, PA

Skillet Taco Salad

2 pounds ground beef
1 medium onion, chopped
1 teaspoon garlic powder
1 package taco seasoning
1 teaspoon cumin
½ cup water
1 pint salsa
1 (15 ounce) can black beans, drained and rinsed
1 (15 ounce) can whole kernel corn, drained
1 (8 ounce) package cream cheese, softened
2 cups sour cream
2 teaspoons cumin
1 package ranch dressing mix
1 teaspoon taco seasoning
½ teaspoon garlic powder
3 cups shredded cheddar cheese, divided
7 ounces lettuce, shredded
3 small tomatoes, chopped
Corn chips, crushed

In a 15-inch cast-iron skillet, brown beef with onion. Season with 1 teaspoon garlic powder, 1 package taco seasoning, and 1 teaspoon cumin. Mix in water. Spread mixture into bottom of pan and remove from heat. Top with salsa, beans, and corn. In a bowl, beat together cream cheese then slowly add sour cream until smooth. Beat in 2 teaspoons cumin, ranch dressing mix, 1 teaspoon taco seasoning, and ½ teaspoon garlic powder. Spread mixture over corn layer. Sprinkle the following on in layers: 2 cups cheese, lettuce, tomatoes, 1 cup cheese, corn chips. Don't let it sit too long before serving (3 hours was almost too long for me).

Brenda Graber, Hamptonville, NC

Cheeseburger Salad

¾ pound ground beef, browned
½ cup chopped dill pickles
¾ cup ketchup
1 tablespoon mustard
Lettuce

Tomatoes, chopped
Onion, chopped
Shredded cheese
Croutons

Mix together beef, pickles, ketchup, and mustard. Layer in bowl starting with lettuce, then beef mixture, tomatoes, onion, cheese, and croutons. Good served with Western Dressing.

Western Dressing:

2 cups Miracle Whip
   salad dressing
1½ cups sugar
¼ cup ketchup
½ cup oil

2 teaspoons mustard
1 teaspoon paprika
4 teaspoons water
½ teaspoon salt
¼ cup vinegar

Mix all together until blended.

Jolene Bontrager, Topeka, IN

Tuna Salad

2 (7 ounce) cans tuna in oil
½ cup minced celery
1 tablespoon minced
   green pepper

1 teaspoon salt
⅛ teaspoon pepper
½ cup mayonnaise
2 teaspoons lemon juice

Mash tuna in a bowl. Add celery, green pepper, salt, pepper, mayonnaise, and lemon juice and mix thoroughly. Makes enough for 6 sandwiches.

Mrs. Melvin (Bertha) Schwartz, Fredericktown, OH

VEGETABLE PIZZA

2 tubes crescent rolls
1 (8 ounce) package
  cream cheese
1 large container sour cream
1½ cups Miracle Whip
  salad dressing
1 to 2 packages ranch
  dressing mix

1 head cauliflower,
  chopped finely
2 bunches broccoli,
  chopped finely
1 onion, chopped finely
Tomato, chopped
Bell pepper, chopped
Shredded cheese

Spread crescent roll dough onto a large cookie sheet, pressing dough together to seal joints. Bake at 350 degrees for 11 minutes. Don't over-bake. Cool. In a bowl, blend cream cheese, sour cream, Miracle Whip, and ranch dressing mix. Spead over cooled crust. Top with cauliflower, broccoli, onion, tomato, pepper, and cheese. Cut into squares to serve.

Mrs. Menno J. Miller, Gallipolis, OH

BAKED CARROTS

A delicious twist on carrots.

2 quarts chopped carrots
1 tablespoon salt
American cheese

¼ cup vinegar
¼ cup browned butter

Cook carrots in salted water until tender. Drain. In a casserole dish, layer carrots and cheese twice. Pour vinegar and butter over top. Bake at 350 degrees for 30 minutes or until heated through.

Lauren Zimmerman, Akron, PA

BEST-EVER CORN CASSEROLE

2 cups whole kernel corn
2 cups cream-style corn
1 small onion, chopped
1 (8 ounce) container sour cream

1 package corn muffin mix
Salt and pepper to taste
Dried parsley

In a bowl, combine all ingredients and pour in a greased casserole. Bake at 350 degrees for 45 minutes. Yields 10 servings.

MARY ELLEN SCHWARTZ, Mayslick, KY

CORN FRITTERS

2 eggs
¼ cup flour
1 teaspoon baking powder
1 teaspoon salt

⅛ teaspoon pepper
2 cups corn, grated from cob
2 tablespoons heavy cream

In a bowl, beat eggs. In another bowl, combine flour, baking powder, salt, and pepper then add corn. Mix in eggs and cream thoroughly. Fry in oil until lightly browned on both sides.

MRS. DANIEL STOLTZFUS, Nottingham, PA

GREEN BEAN DISH
Unusual but delicious!

2 quarts canned green beans
6 ounces cream cheese

10 strips bacon, fried
  and crumbled

Heat beans then drain liquid. Add cream cheese and cover until partially melted. Stir in bacon and serve.

SAM BEILER, Paradise, PA

Grandma's Green Beans

My grandmother made these and I thought they were the best green beans I ever ate.

1 quart fresh snapped
  green beans
Salt to taste
1 cup milk
2 tablespoons flour

2 tablespoons milk
Velveeta cheese, diced
  or shredded
Brown sugar (optional)
Bacon bits (optional)

In a saucepan, boil beans in enough water to cover. Season to taste with salt. When tender, drain water off beans and add 1 cup milk to beans. In a bowl, blend flour with 2 tablespoons milk until smooth. Stir into hot beans and milk, stirring until thickened. If too thick, thin with more milk for a nice sauce. Add Velveeta cheese to your taste. Garnish with brown sugar and bacon bits if desired.

Mary Ann L. Byler, New Wilmington, PA

ONION RINGS

3 large onions
Oil
½ cup milk

1 egg
¾ cup flour
½ teaspoon salt

Cut onions into ¼-inch slices and separate into rings. Heat oil in a saucepan to 375 degrees. In a bowl, combine milk, egg, flour, and salt with a whisk until smooth. Dip each ring into batter and let excess drip off. Fry a few rings at a time in hot oil, turning once, until golden brown, about 2 minutes. Set aside to drain. To keep onion rings warm and prevent sogginess, place in a 300-degree oven until all are done frying and you are ready to serve.

MALINDA GINGERICH, Spartansburg, PA

CREAMED PEAS

⅛ teaspoon baking soda
⅔ cup water
1 pound frozen peas
1 tablespoon sugar
¾ teaspoon salt

¼ teaspoon pepper
3 tablespoons butter
¾ cup milk
1½ teaspoons flour

In a saucepan, dissolve baking soda in water, and add peas, sugar, salt, and pepper. Bring to a boil then add butter. Combine milk and flour in a bowl and stir slowly into peas. Bring to a boil again and cook over medium heat until thick and bubbly, about 5 minutes.

RACHEL BRICKER, Middlefield, OH

Knepfle or Egg Dumplings

3 cups flour
2 teaspoons salt
3 eggs

1 cup water (approximately)
Butter

In a bowl, mix flour and salt. Add eggs and enough water to make a fairly moist, stiff batter. Fill a 4- or 5-quart kettle half full with water and bring to a boil. Take 1 tablespoon batter and use a silver knife to cut off ⅛-inch slices the length of the spoon into boiling water. Dip knife into water often to help with easy slicing. Keep adding sliced batter and stirring often. Let simmer 15 to 20 minutes. Drain dumplings through a colander. In a skillet with butter, fry dumplings until lightly browned. Or, you can serve the dumplings with browned butter.

Mrs. Melvin (Bertha) Schwartz, Fredericktown, OH

Bern Fried Potatoes (Berner Roesti)

*This recipe was printed on a handkerchief brought
from Bern, Switzerland, dating back to 1867.*

Peel potatoes that have been cooked in their skins until tender and chilled. Slice them very thin. Into a boil. Season with salt and sprinkle with a little water or milk. In an iron skillet, melt lard or butter. When hot add potatoes and stir into fat. Then press potatoes down into the pan spreading them thinly and evenly over the bottom. Cover. Fry over medium heat until when pan is shaken the potatoes easily loosen from the bottom. Place plate over the skillet that is at least as big as the skillet. Flip potatoes out of skillet onto the plate.

Mrs. Melvin (Bertha) Schwartz, Fredericktown, OH

Ranch Potato Cubes

7 medium potatoes, cut
  into ½-inch cubes
Salt and pepper to taste
Garlic powder to taste
2 tablespoons butter, melted

2 cups sour cream
1 envelope ranch dressing mix
3 cups shredded cheddar cheese
¾ to 1 pound bacon,
  fried and crumbled

Place potatoes in a 9x13-inch pan and season to taste with salt, pepper, and garlic powder. Dot with butter. Cover with foil and bake at 325 degrees for 1 hour or until tender. In a bowl, combine sour cream and ranch dressing mix. Spread over potatoes. Top with cheese and bacon. Bake uncovered until cheese is melted. A delicious and easy side dish for grilled meat of any kind.

Brenda Graber, Hamptonville, NC

CREAMY MASHED POTATOES

12 large potatoes, peeled
  and cooked
1 (8 ounce) package
  cream cheese

1 cup sour cream
2 teaspoons salt
½ teaspoon garlic salt
½ cup margarine

Mash potatoes. Add cream cheese, sour cream, salt, garlic salt, and margarine; blend well. Spoon into a baking dish and bake at 350 degrees for 1 hour. Mashed potatoes can be frozen until ready to use.

MARTHA YODER, Crofton, KY

White Gravy

¼ cup butter
¾ cup flour

Salt and pepper to taste
4 cups water or milk

In a skillet, melt butter then add flour and stir until lightly browned. Season with salt and pepper to taste. Slowly add water 1 cup at a time, stirring constantly. Keep stirring until gravy thickens. Serve on meat, mashed potatoes, or biscuits.

FANNIE L. STUTZMAN, West Salem, OH

Sloppy Potatoes

3 medium potatoes, sliced
1 medium onion, sliced
1 tablespoon butter

½ teaspoon salt
½ cup water

In a medium saucepan, bring all ingredients to a boil. Reduce to low and cook 15 minutes, stirring occasionally.

Home-Style Scalloped Potatoes

⅓ cup chopped onion
5 tablespoons butter
  or margarine
5 tablespoons flour

1¼ teaspoons salt
½ teaspoon pepper
5 cups milk
6 cups thinly sliced potatoes

In a large saucepan, sauté onion in butter until tender. Stir in flour, salt, and pepper. Gradually add milk. Bring to a boil and cook and stir 2 minutes or until sauce is thickened. Place half of potatoes in a greased 3-quart baking dish. Pour half of sauce over potatoes. Repeat layers. Bake at 350 degrees uncovered for 60 to 70 minutes or until potatoes are tender and top is lightly browned.

LINDA PEACHEY, Beaver, OH

Honey-Glazed Sweet Potatoes

2 pounds sweet potatoes
2 tablespoons butter, melted
1 teaspoon fresh lemon juice
3 tablespoons honey
Salt and pepper to taste

Cut sweet potatoes into ½- to ¾-inch squares. In a bowl, mix butter, lemon juice, honey, salt, and pepper. Pour over sweet potatoes and stir to coat. Place in a baking pan and cover. Bake at 425 degrees for 20 to 30 minutes until potatoes are soft.

Susan Gingerich, Dalton, OH

Pecan Sweet Potato Bake

3 cups mashed sweet potatoes
2 eggs
½ cup sugar
¼ cup half-and-half
¼ cup butter, softened
2 teaspoons vanilla
⅛ teaspoon salt

In a large mixing bowl, combine all ingredients. Beat until light and fluffy. Transfer to a greased 11x7x2-inch baking dish.

Topping:

½ cup brown sugar
2 tablespoons flour
¼ cup cold butter
½ cup chopped pecans

In a bowl, combine brown sugar and flour. Cut in butter until crumbly. Fold in pecans and sprinkle on sweet potato mixture. Bake uncovered at 350 degrees for 30 to 35 minutes.

Mary Miller, North Bloomfield, OH

STUFFED PEPPERS

8 to 10 peppers, hot or
sweet banana
1 (8 ounce) package cream
cheese, softened

1 (8 ounce) bag shredded
cheddar cheese
1 pound sausage, fried
and crumbled
8 to 10 slices bacon

Wash peppers and slice lengthwise, removing seeds. In a bowl, mix cream
cheese, cheddar cheese, and sausage. Fill each pepper with mixture. Wrap
1 slice bacon around each filled pepper and secure with toothpick. Bake at
350 degrees until filling is hot and bacon is crisp.

MALINDA GINGERICH, Spartansburg, PA

MIXED VEGETABLE CASSEROLE

2½ pounds mixed vegetables
1 tablespoon salt
¼ cup butter
½ pound Velveeta cheese

1 can cream of mushroom soup
2 cups crushed Ritz crackers
3 tablespoons butter, melted

In a pot, cook vegetables in salted water until partly soft. Drain. In a sauce-pan, melt ¼ cup butter and add cheese, stirring to melt over low heat. Add soup. Stir in vegetables then place in a baking dish. In a bowl, combine crackers and 3 tablespoons melted butter. Sprinkle over vegetables. Bake uncovered at 350 degrees for 10 to 15 minutes.

Susan Gingerich, Dalton, OH

ZUCCHINI APPETIZER

4 eggs
4 cups grated zucchini
½ cup mozzarella cheese
2 tablespoons parsley
½ cup chopped onion
½ cup oil

½ teaspoon salt
1 cup flour
½ tablespoon baking powder
Sausage, fried
1 can stewed tomatoes, drained
Meltz cheese sauce

In a mixing bowl, mix eggs, zucchini, and cheese. Add parsley, onion, oil, and salt. Mix in flour and baking powder. Spread in a greased 9x13-inch pan and bake at 350 degrees for 45 minutes. Add sausage, tomatoes, and cheese sauce on top.

DELILA YODER, Homerville, OH

ZUCCHINI BAKE

3 cups grated zucchini
1 onion, chopped
½ cup oil
4 eggs
1 cup flour

1 teaspoon baking powder
½ teaspoon garlic
   powder (optional)
1 teaspoon salt
Shredded cheese

Mix all ingredients together, except cheese, and pour into a 9x13-inch casserole pan. Bake at 350 degrees for 30 to 40 minutes until set. When almost done, top with cheese.

MRS. FREEMAN (SYLVIA) MAST, Constable, NY

Amish Dressing

A family favorite!

1 loaf homemade bread
3 cups milk
4 eggs, beaten
1 teaspoon salt
½ teaspoon pepper
1 tablespoon chicken base

1 pint dressing mix
(a combination of
chopped cooked potatoes,
carrots, and celery)
1 cup cooked and diced
chicken with broth
Butter

Cut bread into cubes. Toast in a skillet with a little butter. In a bowl, mix toasted bread with milk, eggs, salt, pepper, chicken base, dressing mix, and chicken. Brown some butter in the bottom of a 9x13-inch pan. Add dressing and bake at 350 to 400 degrees. Flip dressing occasionally until done to your liking.

Mrs. Joseph Miller, Navarre, OH

STICK-TO-YOUR-RIBS MAIN DISHES

Spend your time counting your blessings,
not airing your complaints.

AMISH SAYING

Tortilla Rolls

There are never any leftovers when these are served.

8 ounces sour cream
1 (8 ounce) package
   cream cheese
1 (4 ounce) can diced
   green chilies
½ cup shredded cheddar cheese
½ cup chopped onion
1 envelope ranch dressing mix
⅛ teaspoon salt
⅛ teaspoon seasoned salt
½ pound diced ham
10 tortillas

Mix all together and spread onto tortillas. Roll each up. Secure and chill. Slice before serving. You may choose to add additional diced vegetables like broccoli and carrots.

Mrs. Mae Mast, Holmesville, OH

Buffalo Chicken Dip

2 cups cooked chicken
2 cups shredded cheese
1 (8 ounce) package
   cream cheese
1 cup ranch dressing
½ cup buffalo sauce

Mix all together and bake at 350 degrees for 30 minutes. Serve with tortilla chips.

Amanda Rose Esh, Parkesburg, PA

Hot Pizza Dip

2 (8 ounce) packages cream
  cheese, softened
2 teaspoons Italian seasoning
½ teaspoon garlic powder
4 cups mozzarella cheese

12 ounces pizza sauce
1 to 2 cups pepperoni,
  cut into small pieces
Bacon crumbles

In a bowl, mix cream cheese, Italian seasoning, and garlic powder. Spread into a 9x13-inch pan. Sprinkle half of mozzarella cheese on top. Spread with pizza sauce. Layer with pepperoni, remaining mozzarella cheese, and bacon crumbles. Bake at 350 degrees for 20 minutes. Serve warm with tortilla chips, pretzels, pita chips, and the like.

JUDITH MILLER, Fredericktown, OH

Our Favorite Sausage Dip

1 pound sausage
1 onion, chopped
1 large or 2 small bell
  peppers, chopped

1 package ranch dressing mix
1 can cheddar cheese soup
1 can fiesta nacho cheese soup

In a skillet, brown sausage, onion, and bell pepper together. Add dressing mix, cheddar cheese soup, and nacho cheese soup. Mix well and heat through. Serve with tortilla chips.

ADEN AND ROSE TROYER, Burton, OH

Taco Dip

8 ounces cream cheese, softened
16 ounces sour cream
2 packages taco seasoning
¼ cup sugar (optional)
1 pound ground beef

2 tablespoons brown sugar
1 tablespoon ketchup
Lettuce, shredded
Cheese, shredded

In a bowl, blend cream cheese, sour cream, 1 package taco seasoning, and sugar; spread into the bottom of a 9x9-inch pan. In a skillet, brown beef and mix in 1 package taco seasoning, brown sugar, and ketchup. Cool. Spread over bottom layer. Top with lettuce and cheese. Serve with tortilla chips.

Dora Coblentz, Greenfield, OH

Easy Pizza Sandwiches

Bread slices
Butter
1 hamburger, crumbled
  beef, or meat of choice

Pizza sauce
Cheese, sliced or shredded

Butter 1 side of bread slice and put butter-side down on a cookie sheet. Spread pizza sauce on bread. Layer with meat and cheese. Bake at 350 degrees for 10 to 15 minutes until cheese is melted and bread is slightly crisp around the edges.

Eli and Laura Petersheim, Kenton, OH

Ham and Cheese Sticky Buns

2 (12 count) packages
  Hawaiian dinner rolls
1 pound thinly sliced ham
1 pound or more Swiss cheese
1 cup butter

2 tablespoons
  Worcestershire sauce
2 tablespoons poppy seeds
2 tablespoons mustard
⅓ cup brown sugar

Remove dinner rolls from package without breaking apart individual rolls. Slice whole group of rolls in half and set bottom half in 2 greased 9x13-inch pans. Layer with ham and cheese. Cover with top layer of rolls. In a saucepan, combine butter, Worcestershire sauce, poppy seeds, mustard, and brown sugar until dissolved into a sauce. Pour over and between rolls. Bake uncovered at 350 degrees for 20 minutes. Cut apart and serve.

Amos and Elizabeth Wengerd, Monroe, IN

Runza Buns

Dough:

1 tablespoon yeast
½ cup warm water
¾ cup lukewarm milk
¼ cup sugar
¼ cup shortening

1 egg
1 teaspoon salt
2 cups whole-wheat flour
2 cups all-purpose flour

In a mixing bowl, dissolve yeast in warm water and lukewarm milk. Add sugar and shortening, stirring until melted. Beat in egg and salt. Slowly work in flours. Cover and let dough rise until double in size.

Filling:

1½ pounds ground beef
5 cups shredded cabbage
⅔ cup water
½ cup ketchup

¾ cup barbecue sauce
1 teaspoon salt
16 slices cheese

In a skillet, brown beef and drain grease. In a saucepan, cook cabbage in water for 15 minutes; drain. Add beef, ketchup, barbecue sauce, and salt; mix well. Divide dough into 16 pieces and roll out into 5- to 6-inch circles. Top each circle with slice of cheese. Divide filling evenly between circles. Bring edges of dough up over filling to center. Pinch edges to seal. Place seam-side down on baking sheet and let rise for about 20 minutes. Bake at 400 degrees for 12 to 15 minutes.

Dorcas Marie Yoder, Meyersdale, PA

PIGS IN A BLANKET

2 cups flour, divided
2 tablespoons sugar
½ teaspoon salt
1½ teaspoons yeast
2 tablespoons soft butter

¼ cup warm water
¼ cup warm milk
1 small egg
1 package Little
  Smokies sausages

In a medium bowl, mix together 1 cup flour, sugar, salt, and yeast. Add butter, water, milk, and egg. Mix thoroughly. Add remaining flour and knead until smooth. Let rise for 1 hour or until doubled in size. Divide dough into 4 parts. Roll out each part into an 8-inch circle. Cut into wedges. Place 1 smokie on widest end and roll up dough around it. Bake on cookie sheet at 350 degrees for 12 to 15 minutes. Serve with ketchup or honey mustard.

KARI PETERSHEIM, Fredericktown, OH

BBQ HAM

¾ cup brown sugar
½ scant cup flour
24 ounces ketchup
2 cups barbecue sauce

4 teaspoons mustard
½ cup maple syrup (optional)
10 pounds chipped ham

In a large mixing bowl, mix brown sugar and flour before adding ketchup, barbecue sauce, mustard, and maple syrup. Mix in ham, coating well. Place in a roasting pan. Place in a 350-degree oven for 20 to 30 minutes until heated through. Serve on bread or buns.

MENNO J. YODERS, Berlin, PA

Sloppy Sandwiches

1 pound ground beef
½ small onion, chopped
½ teaspoon garlic, minced

1 (10 ounce) can cream
soup (chicken,
mushroom, or celery)
12 hamburger buns

Brown beef, onion, and garlic. Add soup and simmer until thickened. Serve on buns.

Sloppy Joes

1½ pounds ground beef
3 tablespoons chopped onion
3 tablespoons vinegar
2 tablespoons barbecue sauce
1 cup water

1 cup ketchup
3 tablespoons brown sugar
Salt and pepper to taste
½ cup oatmeal
Hamburger buns

In a skillet, brown beef and onion; drain. Add vinegar, barbecue sauce, water, ketchup, brown sugar, salt, and pepper; bring to a boil. Simmer 30 minutes. Add oatmeal and simmer 15 more minutes. Serve on buns.

FANNIE L. STUTZMAN, West Salem, OH

Sweet and Sour Meatballs

3 pounds ground beef
1 cup chopped onion
1 cup milk
2 cups quick oats
Salt and pepper to taste

1 cup ketchup
½ cup vinegar
2 tablespoons
  Worcestershire sauce
2 tablespoons brown sugar

Preheat oven to 350 degrees. Mix ground beef, onion, milk, and oats. Season with salt and pepper. Shape mixture into balls and place in a shallow baking pan. In a bowl, combine ketchup, vinegar, Worcestershire sauce, and brown sugar. Pour sauce over meatballs. Bake for 30 to 40 minutes.

Emma Eicher, Geneva, IN

Little Cheddar Meat Loaves

1 egg
¾ cup milk
1 cup shredded cheddar cheese
½ cup quick oats
½ cup chopped onion

1 teaspoon salt
1 pound lean ground beef
⅔ cup ketchup
½ cup brown sugar
1½ teaspoons mustard

In a bowl, beat egg and milk. Stir in cheese, oats, onion, and salt. Add beef; mix well. Shape into 8 small loaves and place in a lightly greased 9x13-inch pan. In a small bowl, mix ketchup, brown sugar, and mustard. Spoon over each loaf. Bake, uncovered, at 350 degrees for 45 minutes or until done. Yields 8 servings.

Mrs. Menno J. Miller, Gallipolis, OH

Poor Man's Steak

3 pounds ground beef
1 cup cracker crumbs
1 cup water
2 teaspoons salt

Pepper to taste
Flour
Oil
1 can cream of mushroom soup

Mix ground beef, cracker crumbs, water, salt, and pepper. Pat mixture into a 10x15-inch jelly roll pan. Refrigerate overnight. Cut into 12 squares. Coat with flour and brown in oil on both sides. Place in a casserole pan and top with mushroom soup. Bake at 350 degrees for 1 hour.

Mrs. Menno J. Miller, Gallipolis, OH

Mushroom Swiss Steak

½ cup flour
2 teaspoons salt
½ teaspoon pepper

2½ pounds round steak,
   1½ inch thick
2 to 3 tablespoons fat
   or shortening
1 can cream of mushroom soup

Combine flour, salt, and pepper. Coat both sides of steak with flour mixture. Pound meat on both sides with a mallet until all flour is absorbed. In a skillet, melt fat. When hot, place steak in pan and brown well on both sides. Turn heat to lowest setting and add soup. Cover and simmer 1 hour. Serves 3 to 4.

Mrs. Melvin (Bertha) Schwartz, Fredericktown, OH

Pepper Steak

1 medium onion, sliced
2 green peppers, cut in strips
2 tablespoons butter
2 pounds steak, cut in slices
1½ cups water

1 tablespoon brown sugar
Salt and pepper to taste
2 tablespoons cornstarch
Soy sauce to taste

In a skillet, sauté onion and peppers in butter. Remove from pan. Add steak to pan and brown on both sides. Add water, brown sugar, salt and pepper, and cornstarch. Return onion and peppers to pan. Drizzle with soy sauce to taste. Serve with rice or mashed potatoes. I do this with my own canned steak and broth in place of water.

LOVINA GINGERICH, Dalton, OH

Cured Ham

2 cups salt
½ cup brown sugar

2 tablespoons pepper
1 tablespoon red pepper

Mix all ingredients in a bowl then rub onto your uncured ham. Wrap ham in cheesecloth and hang to cure in the basement for 4 weeks. Slice ham and cook in your favorite way. We like to cook with green beans, carrots, and potatoes.

VERNA D. GINGERICH, Mount Ayr, IA

Pot Roast with Mushroom Gravy

1 (3½ pound) boneless beef roast
2 large cloves garlic,
　thinly sliced
1 teaspoon salt
1 teaspoon garlic salt
1 teaspoon pepper
¼ cup flour
3 tablespoons oil

2 cups brewed coffee
1 can cream of mushroom soup
1 tablespoon
　Worcestershire sauce
1 large onion, sliced
3 tablespoons cornstarch
3 tablespoons water

Cut slits in roast with a sharp knife. Push 1 slice garlic into each slit. Sprinkle roast with salts and pepper. Lightly dredge in flour, patting off excess flour. Brown roast on all sides in hot oil in a large Dutch oven. Blend coffee, soup, and Worcestershire sauce and pour over roast; top with onion. Cover and simmer for 3 hours or until tender. Reserve drippings to make gravy. Combine cornstarch and water. Stir into drippings. Bring mixture to a boil and cook for 1 minute or until thickened. Pour gravy over roast.

Barbara Miller, Camden Wyoming, DE

Golden Baked Chicken

6 chicken breasts, cut up
½ cup flour
½ teaspoon salt
Dash pepper
½ teaspoon paprika

¼ cup butter, melted
1 can cream of chicken soup
¼ cup water
1 tablespoon minced parsley

Coat chicken with mixture of flour, salt, pepper, and paprika. Arrange chicken in a single layer in a buttered shallow baking dish. Drizzle melted butter over chicken. Bake at 375 degrees for 20 minutes. Turn chicken over and bake 20 minutes longer. Mix cream of chicken soup with ¼ cup water and pour over chicken. Sprinkle with parsley. Bake an additional 20 minutes.

EDNA NISLEY, Baltic, OH

Poppy Seed Chicken

6 cups cooked and chopped
  chicken or turkey
2 cups sour cream
2 (10.75 ounce) cans cream
  of chicken soup

3 cups (2 sleeves) crushed
  Ritz crackers
1 cup butter, melted
1 to 2 tablespoons poppy seeds

Mix chicken, sour cream, and soup together and place in a large casserole pan. In a bowl, mix crackers and butter. Spread over chicken mixture. Sprinkle with poppy seeds. Bake at 350 degrees for 40 minutes.

ESTHER J. GINGERICH, Fredericksburg, OH

Chicken Noodles

2 (50 ounce) cans cream
  of chicken soup
4 (48 ounce) containers
  chicken broth

½ cup chicken base
1 pound butter, browned
5 pounds noodles
2 pounds Velveeta cheese

In a large stockpot, bring soup, broth, and chicken base to a boil. Add butter and noodles. Fill pot to three-quarters full with added water. Return to a boil. Turn off burner. Let sit covered for 1 hour. Add cheese and stir in.

FANNIE MILLER, Cass City, MI

Biscuits and Chicken Gravy

This was a childhood favorite, and I was always excited
to hear when it was for supper. Very delicious! So, now
I enjoy making it for my family who also love it.

BISCUITS:

2 cups flour
2½ teaspoons baking powder
½ teaspoon salt
⅓ cup coconut oil or shortening
¾ cup milk

In a bowl, sift together flour, baking powder, and salt. Cut in coconut oil until crumbly. Mix in milk to form a dough. Knead like you would pie dough and cut into small biscuits. Place on an ungreased baking sheet. Bake at 475 degrees for 12 to 15 minutes.

GRAVY:

1 tablespoon minced
  onion (optional)
4 tablespoons butter, bacon
  grease, or chicken fat
4 tablespoons flour
2 cups chicken broth with
  drippings from baked
  or fried chicken
1 cup milk
½ teaspoon salt
Pepper to taste
2 to 3 cups chopped
  leftover chicken

In a large skillet, cook onion in butter until onion softens. Stir in flour to form a paste and cook 2 minutes, stirring constantly until it bubbles a bit, but don't let it brown. Whisk in broth and milk. Keep whisking until mixture is smooth and thickens to desired consistency. Season with salt and pepper. Mix in chicken and stir until chicken is warmed through. Serve hot over hot biscuits.

MARY MILLER, Junction City, OH

CHICKEN LASAGNA

1 (10.5 ounce) can cream
  of chicken soup
1 (10.5 ounce) can cream
  of mushroom soup
¼ cup mayonnaise
¼ cup heavy cream

1 pound chicken, cooked
  and chopped
½ cup grated Parmesan cheese
2 cups grated mozzarella
  cheese, divided
9 lasagna noodles, parboiled

In a bowl, mix chicken soup, mushroom soup, mayonnaise, cream, chicken, Parmesan cheese, and 1 cup mozzarella cheese. In a casserole dish, place 3 noodles and top with half of mixture. Top with 3 noodles and remaining mixture. Top with last 3 noodles and 1 cup mozzarella cheese. Bake at 375 degrees for 45 minutes.

ANNA FISHER, Coatesville, PA

CHICKEN BROCCOLI CASSEROLE

3⅓ cups chicken broth or water
2 cups rice
4 cups chopped broccoli
1½ cups diced carrots
1 cup chopped onion
⅓ cup chicken or turkey fat

⅔ cup flour
1 quart broth
2 scant teaspoons salt
½ teaspoon pepper
4 cups chopped cooked chicken

In a kettle, bring broth to a boil. Add rice and bring to a boil again. Turn heat to low, cover, and cook for 30 minutes. Meanwhile, in a saucepan, steam broccoli, carrots, and onion in a little water until just tender. In another saucepan, melt fat and stir in flour. Add broth, salt, and pepper. Bring to a boil, stirring with a whisk until thickened. Combine rice, drained vegetables, chicken, and sauce and place in a casserole pan or roaster. Bake at 350 degrees for 35 minutes or until hot through.

ESTHER L. MILLER, Fredericktown, OH

Grilled Chicken Alfredo

Boneless chicken breasts
Tender Quick curing salt blend
Zesty Italian dressing
Pasta of choice

Day 1, trim fat from chicken. Sprinkle with Tender Quick and refrigerate for 1 day. Day 2, wash each piece of chicken. Place in a container and coat with zesty Italian dressing. Refrigerate for 2 days. Grill chicken to your liking and slice. Prepare your pasta of choice.

Alfredo:

¼ cup butter
2 teaspoons minced garlic
1½ teaspoons salt
1½ teaspoons pepper
1 teaspoon basil
1 tablespoon lemon juice
1½ cups heavy whipping cream
2 (8 ounce) packages
 cream cheese
½ cup Parmesan cheese
1 package ranch dressing mix

In a kettle, melt butter and gently sauté garlic with salt, pepper, and basil. Add lemon juice and cream. Add cream cheese and stir to melt. Add Parmesan cheese and ranch dressing mix. Serve Alfredo with pasta and chicken.

BRENDA GRABER, Hamptonville, NC

Chicken and Filling

1 chicken, boiled or
 baked and deboned
8 to 10 cups bread cubes
2 medium onions, chopped
½ cup shredded carrots or
 chopped sweet peppers
½ cup diced celery (optional)
1 teaspoon salt
1 teaspoon pepper
2 teaspoons paprika
1 cup chicken broth

Combine all ingredients and pour into a baking dish. Bake at 300 degrees for 1 hour. Serve with gravy.

Chicken Dumplings

2 cups chopped mixed
   vegetables (potatoes, carrots,
   celery, and onions)
1 cup chopped chicken

Water
Salt and chicken
   flavoring to taste

Cook vegetables until soft. Place chicken in a 3-quart saucepan and cover with water; add salt and chicken flavoring. Heat to boiling and cook until chicken is done. Add vegetables and bring back to a boil before adding dumpling dough.

Dumplings:

1½ cups flour
⅓ cup butter, softened
1 teaspoon salt

2 teaspoons baking powder
2 teaspoons sugar
Milk

Combine flour, butter, salt, baking powder, and sugar. Add enough milk to make a stiff dough. Drop by spoonfuls in boiling chicken mixture. Cover and reduce heat for 20 minutes without lifting lid.

Ada Miller, Norwalk, WI

Lisa Martin, Shippensburg, PA

Mom's Galoushka
(German Stuffed Cabbage Rolls)

1 large head cabbage
1 to 2 tablespoons apple
    cider vinegar
1 cup cooked rice
    (white or brown)

1 pound ground beef
¼ pound ground pork
½ teaspoon salt
¼ teaspoon pepper
2 (15 ounce) cans tomato sauce

Place cabbage in a kettle with just enough water to cover bottom of pan. Add apple cider vinegar to water. Cover kettle and steam until cabbage leaves turn a light color. Remove cabbage from kettle to cool. In a large bowl, combine cooked rice, ground beef, ground pork, salt, and pepper. Mix well and form mixture into small balls, then roll in cooled cabbage leaves. Place in a roasting pan and cover with tomato sauce. May add some water to bottom of pan for more moisture. Cover and bake at 350 degrees for 1½ hours. Good served with mashed potatoes.

Wanda E. Brunstetter

French Fry Casserole

1 bag frozen french
  fries, cut smaller
2 cups sour cream
1 package ranch dressing mix

1 to 2 cups cooked,
  chopped chicken
½ cup fried, crumbled bacon
1 cup shredded cheese

In a baking dish, place fries. Mix sour cream and dressing mix; pour over fries. Put a layer of chicken over fries, then a layer of bacon and cheese. Bake at 350 degrees for 30 to 40 minutes until done.

LINDA YODER, New Wilmington, PA

Beef and Noodle Casserole

1½ pounds ground beef
1 tablespoon butter
  or margarine
1 large onion, chopped
1 cup chopped green pepper
1 tablespoon
  Worcestershire sauce

1 (10 ounce) package wide
  noodles, cooked and drained
2 (10¾ ounce) cans cream
  of tomato soup
1 (10¾ ounce) can cream
  of mushroom soup
4 ounces cheddar
  cheese, shredded

Brown beef in a large skillet. Remove beef and drain fat. In same skillet, melt butter over medium-high heat. Sauté onion and pepper until tender. Add beef, Worcestershire sauce, noodles, and soups. Mix well. Spoon into a greased 3-quart casserole and top with cheese. Bake at 350 degrees for 45 minutes. Yield: 8 servings.

JUDITH MARTIN, Millmont, PA

Underground Ham Casserole

4 cups chopped ham
4 tablespoons butter
⅓ cup chopped onion
2 tablespoons
   Worcestershire sauce
3 to 4 quarts mashed potatoes
   made with 1 pint sour cream
   instead of milk and butter

2 cans cream of mushroom soup
3 cups milk
2 cups shredded cheese
8 to 10 strips bacon,
   fried and crumbled

In a saucepan, place ham, butter, onion, and Worcestershire sauce and simmer for 10 minutes. Pour into a large casserole dish or roasting pan. Top with mashed potatoes. In a saucepan, mix soup and milk, stirring until warmed. Pour over potatoes. Top with cheese then bacon. Bake at 350 degrees for 30 minutes until slightly browned and heated through.

ESTHER J. GINGERICH, Fredericksburg, OH

Scalloped Potatoes and Pork Chops

5 cups peeled and thinly
   sliced potatoes
1 cup chopped onion
Salt and pepper to taste

1 can cream of mushroom soup
½ cup sour cream
6 pork loin chops (1 inch thick)
Chopped fresh parsley

Preheat oven to 375 degrees. In a greased 9x13-inch baking pan, layer half the potatoes and onion and sprinkle with salt and pepper. Repeat layer. Combine soup and sour cream and pour over potato mixture. Cover and bake for 30 minutes. Meanwhile, in a skillet, brown pork chops on both sides. Place pork chops on top of casserole. Cover and return to oven for 45 minutes or until pork chops are tender. Uncover during last 15 minutes of baking. Sprinkle with parsley. Yields 6 servings.

MRS. ENOS CHRISTNER, Bryant, IN

Frankfurter Bake

2 cups macaroni	½ teaspoon salt
2 cups shredded cheese	1 pound hot dogs, sliced
1 cup milk	¼ cup brown sugar
¼ cup butter	¼ cup mayonnaise
2 tablespoons flour	2 tablespoons prepared mustard

Cook macaroni as directed on package. Drain and stir in cheese, milk, butter, flour, and salt. Pour macaroni mixture into a baking dish. In a saucepan, combine brown sugar, mayonnaise, and mustard. Add hot dogs and bring to a boil. Mix into macaroni mixture. Bake at 350 degrees for 25 minutes. Yield: 6 to 8 servings.

LINDA FISHER, Millheim, PA

CHICKEN, HAM, OR BEEF CASSEROLE

*I always like to take this casserole to the
sick or anyone who needs cheering up.*

2 cups diced cooked
 chicken, ham, or beef
2 cups macaroni
2 medium onions, chopped

1 cup frozen peas
2 small cans cream of
 mushroom soup
½ pound shredded cheese

In a bowl, mix meat, macaroni, onions, peas, and soup. Pour into a casserole pan. Cover and refrigerate overnight. Bring pan to room temperature and bake at 350 degrees for 40 to 60 minutes. While baking, give a couple of stirs. In the last 15 to 20 minutes, stir in some cheese and top casserole with the rest.

MARY E. STOLTZFUS, Loysville, PA

SIMPLE TACO DISH

2 cups flour
1 tablespoon baking powder
2 teaspoons sugar
½ teaspoon cream of tartar
½ teaspoon salt
⅔ cup milk
½ cup melted butter
8 ounces cream cheese

16 ounces sour cream
1½ to 2 pounds ground beef
1 package taco seasoning
2 cups pizza sauce
Shredded cheese
Lettuce
Salsa
Tomatoes, chopped

In a mixing bowl, combine flour, baking powder, sugar, cream of tartar, and salt. Mix in milk and butter until just combined. Press into a 9x13-inch pan. Bake at 400 degrees for 15 to 20 minutes. In a saucepan, blend cream cheese and sour cream, heating it just a little. Spread over biscuit crust. In a skillet, fry ground beef, drain excess fat, then season with taco seasoning. Mix in pizza sauce. Put onto sour cream layer. Top with cheese. Bake just until cheese is melted. Serve with lettuce, salsa, and tomatoes.

DORETTA MAST, LaGrange, IN

Green Beans and Sausage

*This is what my dad would make for a
meal when my mom wasn't home.*

Put butter or oil in a frying pan. Drain a can of green beans and place
them in the pan. Add cooked sausage. Fry this together. Serve with ketchup
on top.

Mary Ann L. Byler, New Wilmington, PA

Zucchini Surprise

1 pound ground beef
4 cups shredded zucchini
1 small onion, chopped
3 eggs, beaten
1½ cups cracker crumbs
½ cup milk

½ cup butter, melted
1 teaspoon salt
½ teaspoon pepper
1 cup pizza sauce
1 pound cheese, grated

In a skillet, brown beef; set aside when done. In a bowl, mix zucchini, onion,
eggs, and cracker crumbs; stir well. Add milk, butter, salt, and pepper. Pour
into a greased 9x13-inch pan. Top with beef. Bake at 325 degrees for 50
minutes. Top with pizza sauce and cheese. Bake for 10 minutes.

Mrs. Melvin Schlabach, Dayton, PA

ZUCCHINI OR POTATO CASSEROLE

6 eggs
½ cup oil
1 cup flour
1 tablespoon baking powder
1 teaspoon salt
½ teaspoon pepper
2 tablespoons parsley

2 teaspoons pizza or
  Italian seasoning
½ cup chopped onion
4 cups shredded zucchini
  or potatoes
1 pound sausage or ground beef
Green peppers, chopped
Mushrooms

In a bowl, beat eggs and oil. Add flour, baking powder, salt, pepper, parsley, and pizza seasoning and mix well. Stir in onion, zucchini or potatoes, sausage, green peppers, and mushrooms. Pour into a greased 9x13-inch pan. Bake at 350 degrees for 45 minutes.

ELLA SHETLER, West Salem, OH

Zucchini Pizza

2 cups shredded
  zucchini, drained
2 eggs
2 rounded tablespoons
  mayonnaise
2 tablespoons butter, melted
½ cup crushed saltine crackers

1 teaspoon salt
1 teaspoon sour cream
  and onion powder
Pizza sauce
Shredded mozzarella cheese
Pepperoni and other toppings

In a bowl, mix zucchini and eggs. Add mayonnaise, butter, crackers, salt, and sour cream and onion powder. Mix well. Place in a greased 9x13-inch baking dish. Bake at 350 degrees for 20 minutes until it starts to brown. Top with pizza sauce, cheese, pepperoni, and other desired toppings. Bake approximately 10 minutes until cheese melts and toppings are heated through.

Note: The zucchini mixture can also be fried as patties in hot oil.

Mrs. Jonathan Stoltzfus, Peach Bottom, PA

Easy Pizza Casserole

I usually take this casserole to family gatherings, and it is a big hit.

2 cans cream of mushroom soup
6 cups cooked homemade
 noodles
2 quarts pizza sauce
4 cups fried sausage crumbles
2 cans mushrooms, drained

2 cups shredded cheese
 (I like Colby)
1 cup chopped onion
1 cup chopped green pepper
Pepperoni
Olives

In a roaster pan, spread contents of 1 can soup on bottom. Layer on 3 cups noodles. Pour 1 quart pizza sauce over noodles. Add layer of 2 cups sausage crumbles and 1 can mushrooms, then 1 cup cheese, ½ cup onion, and ½ cup green pepper. Layer on some pepperoni and some olives. Repeat layers with remaining ingredients. Bake at 375 degrees for 1 hour.

Mrs. Martin A. Schmidt, Carlisle, KY

Onion Herb Pizza

1 (8 ounce) package cream
 cheese, softened
1 tablespoon Italian seasoning
1 teaspoon basil
1 teaspoon parsley
½ teaspoon oregano
2 teaspoons garlic salt
1 large onion, chopped

2 to 3 tablespoons butter
½ pound sausage
Your favorite pizza crust, baked
Parmesan cheese, grated
Swiss cheese, shredded
8 ounces shredded
 mozzarella cheese

In a bowl, mix cream cheese, Italian seasoning, basil, parsley, oregano, and garlic salt. In a skillet, sauté onion in butter until lightly browned. Add to cream cheese mixture. In the skillet, brown sausage. Add sausage to cream cheese mixture and spread over pizza crust. Sprinkle generously with Parmesan cheese. Add a thin layer of Swiss cheese. Top with mozzarella cheese. Bake at 350 degrees for 10 to 12 minutes until cheese is melted.

Malinda Gingerich, Spartansburg, PA

HOAGIE PIZZA

1 cup warm water
1 tablespoon yeast
2 tablespoons oil
½ teaspoon salt
1 teaspoon sugar
Dash fresh or dried
    herbs (optional)
2¼ cups flour

Toppings:
Mayonnaise
Mustard
Chipped ham
1½ to 2 cups shredded cheese
Lettuce, thinly sliced
Tomatoes, sliced or diced
Onions, chopped
Peppers, chopped
Cucumbers, sliced or chopped

In a mixing bowl, combine warm water, yeast, oil, salt, and sugar, stirring until dissolved. Add herbs. Work flour in until a stiff dough forms. Let sit 10 minutes. Spread dough on a jelly roll pan; let rise 10 minutes. Bake at 350 degrees for 12 to 15 minutes. Do not overbake. Cool. Add toppings starting with mayonnaise, mustard, ham, and then cheese. Bake at 350 degrees until cheese melts. Remove from oven then add fresh vegetables to the top.

MRS. MELVIN SCHLABACH, Dayton, PA

BARBARA'S HOAGIE PIZZA

So good on a warm summer night with a cold glass of lemonade.

2 (8 ounce) packages cream
    cheese, softened, or 16
    ounces sour cream
1 cup salad dressing or
    mayonnaise (omit if
    using sour cream)
1 package ranch dressing mix

Your favorite pizza crust,
    baked and cooled
Deli ham, chopped
Cheese, shredded
Lettuce, shredded
Tomatoes, chopped
Onions, chopped

In a bowl, blend cream cheese, salad dressing, and ranch dressing mix. Spread over crust. Top with ham, cheese, lettuce, tomatoes, and onions, or other favorite toppings.

BARBARA MILLER, Constable, NY

Pizza Pockets

2 tablespoons yeast
1½ cups warm water
6 tablespoons brown sugar
4½ cups bread flour
Pizza sauce

Cooked meat (ground
  beef, sausage, smokies,
  and/or pepperoni)
Mozzarella cheese
2 teaspoons baking soda
Oregano
Melted butter

Dissolve yeast in water. Add brown sugar. Vigorously stir in flour. Let rise. Roll out dough and cut in wide strips. Spread pizza sauce on center of each strip. Top with meat and cheese. Fold dough over filling and pinch edges. Cut away any extra dough on ends. Dissolve baking soda in a bowl of water. Dip pockets in soda water. Place on a greased baking sheet and sprinkle with oregano. Bake at 400 degrees for 25 to 30 minutes until light brown. Brush with melted butter.

MARY SCHWARTZ, Berne, IN
MRS. BENJAMIN WICKEY, Monroe, IN

Dandelion Gravy

½ pound bacon
⅔ cup flour
3½ cups milk
½ cup sugar
1 teaspoon salt
1½ tablespoons mustard

2 tablespoons vinegar
3 hard-boiled eggs, chopped
4 cups chopped
   dandelion greens
Potatoes, boiled

In a skillet, fry bacon until crisp. Set aside. Add flour to bacon fat and stir until smooth. Slowly add milk and bring to a boil. Add sugar, salt, mustard, and vinegar. Place crumbled bacon, chopped eggs, and chopped greens in a bowl. Just before serving, pour gravy over top. Serve with boiled potatoes.

Malinda Gingerich, Spartansburg, PA

Potato Haystack

10 medium potatoes,
   cooked and chunked
2 packages ranch dressing mix
2 cups sour cream
1 cup milk

½ cup melted butter
4 pounds ground beef
1 package taco seasoning
Velveeta cheese, sliced
Doritos chips, crushed

In a bowl, mix potatoes, ranch dressing mix, sour cream, milk, and butter, stirring to coat potatoes. Place in a large casserole dish. In a large skillet, fry ground beef. When done, mix in taco seasoning. Spoon over potatoes. Top with a layer of sliced Velveeta cheese. Bake at 350 degrees for 30 minutes or until hot through. Top with crushed chips before serving.

Malinda Gingerich, Spartansburg, PA

GOULASH

1 cup elbow macaroni
Boiling water
1 pound ground beef
1 medium onion, chopped
2 cups chopped celery
1 (2 ounce) can mushrooms,
  undrained
1 green pepper, chopped
1 (15 ounce) can tomato sauce
  or 3 cups tomato juice
½ cup ketchup
1 teaspoon salt
¼ teaspoon pepper
1 cup water

Place macaroni in a small bowl. Cover with boiling water; let sit. While macaroni blanches, cook ground beef and onion in a heavy saucepan. Drain fat. Drain macaroni and add to meat along with celery, mushrooms, pepper, tomato sauce, ketchup, seasonings, and water. Mix thoroughly. Cover and simmer 30 minutes, stirring occasionally.

EDNA D. STUTZMAN, Clare, MI

GARBAGE FRIES

1½ to 2 pounds cooked
  french fries
1 batch sloppy joe meat
1 medium green
  pepper, julienned
Hot peppers (optional)
1 batch cheese sauce
Bacon, fried and crumbled

Prepare each plate starting with a pile of french fries. Top with sloppy joe meat, green pepper, hot peppers, cheese sauce, and bacon. Delicious and filling.

MRS. REUBEN (MARTHA) BYLER, Atlantic, PA

Baked Macaroni and Cheese

3 quarts water
1½ teaspoons salt
8 ounces (about 2
cups) macaroni
1 teaspoon salt
½ teaspoon mustard

¼ teaspoon pepper
8 ounces sharp cheddar
cheese, grated
2 cups milk
4 eggs

In a pot, bring water and 1½ teaspoons salt to a boil; add macaroni. Stir to prevent clumping and simmer for 8 minutes. In a small bowl, combine 1 teaspoon salt, mustard, and pepper. Drain macaroni when done. Return to empty pot. Add cheese, seasoning mixture, milk, and eggs. Butter a 2-quart casserole and pour macaroni in. Bake at 350 degrees for 1 hour. Yield: 6 to 8 servings.

Judy Zimmerman, East Earl, PA

Recipe for Happiness

2 heaping cups of patience
1 heartful of love
2 handfuls of generosity

Dash of laughter
1 headful of understanding

Sprinkle generously with kindness. Add plenty of faith and hope. Mix well. Spread over a period of a lifetime. Serve generously to everyone you meet.

Lizzie Ann Swartzentruber, Newcomerstown, OH

COMFORTING SOUPS

If you still have your mother, father, husband, wife, or family, treat them with gentle care, for you never know their value until you see their empty chair.

AMISH SAYING

Toast Soup

*This soup is delicious and soothing on a
cold day or when you are feeling sick.*

2 medium potatoes, chopped
1 medium carrot, chopped
1 small onion, chopped
2 tablespoons butter

8 cups milk
Seasoning and salt to taste
Bread

In a saucepan, cook potatoes, carrot, and onion in a bit of water until softened. In another saucepan, brown butter and whisk in milk. Add cooked vegetables and season to taste. Serve over hot toasted bread.

MARY MILLER, Junction City, OH

Cheddar Chowder Soup

¼ cup butter
¼ cup flour
2 to 3 cups milk
2 cups grated cheddar cheese

1 cup cubed ham or
    meat of choice
1 quart Amish dressing
    mix (potatoes, carrots,
    celery, and onion)

In a saucepan, make white sauce by melting butter. Add flour and stir about 1 minute until smooth. Slowly add milk and cook until thickened. Add cheese and stir until melted. Add ham and dressing mix. Heat through. Serves 6.

ELIZABETH YODER, Kenton, OH

Cheddar Chowder

2 cups water
2 cups diced potatoes
½ cup diced carrots
½ cup diced celery
¼ cup chopped onion
1 teaspoon salt

¼ teaspoon pepper
¼ cup butter
¼ cup flour
2 cups milk
2 cups shredded cheese
1 cup cooked, chopped ham

In a kettle, combine water, potatoes, carrots, celery, onion, salt, and pepper and cook until soft. To make white sauce in a saucepan, melt butter and mix in flour to make a smooth paste. Slowly add milk and cook until thickened. Add cheese, stirring until melted. Add white sauce and ham to vegetables (do not drain vegetables). Serve hot.

RUTH STOLTZFUS, Newburg, PA

AMISH CORN CHOWDER

4 slices bacon
2 tablespoons diced onion
1 tablespoon diced celery
1 tablespoon diced sweet pepper
2 cups corn

2 potatoes, diced
3 tomatoes, chopped
Salt and pepper to taste
2 quarts milk
Chopped parsley

Dice bacon and put into a pan to brown; add onion, celery, and pepper; fry until bacon is crisp. Add corn and fry together for 3 minutes. Add potatoes and tomatoes and season with salt and pepper. Cover and simmer for 30 minutes. Add milk, heat to boiling, then remove from heat. Top with chopped parsley.

Our Favorite Potato Soup

7 cups cubed potatoes
3 stalks celery, chopped
1 medium onion, chopped
⅔ stick butter

1 can beef consommé
2 quarts milk
1 tablespoon salt
½ teaspoon pepper

In a saucepan, cook potatoes in a small amount of water until just tender. In a skillet, sauté celery and onion in butter until clear in color. Do not brown. Add celery and onion to potatoes along with consommé, milk, salt, and pepper. Heat, but do not boil. Makes 15 1-cup servings.

Mrs. Melvin (Bertha) Schwartz, Fredericktown, OH

Potato Soup

4 cups diced potatoes
2 cups chunked ham
1 stalk celery, chopped
½ cup chopped onion
1 large carrot, chopped
½ teaspoon Worcestershire
   sauce

1 tablespoon butter
1 can cream of mushroom soup
2 teaspoons parsley flakes
Seasoned salt
Pepper
Milk
Velveeta cheese

In a large pot, cook potatoes, ham, celery, onion, carrot, Worcestershire sauce, and butter in a little water until tender. Add mushroom soup, parsley, seasoned salt, and pepper to taste. Cover with milk. When milk is hot, add Velveeta to taste and stir until melted.

Malinda Gingerich, Spartansburg, PA

Potato Bacon Chowder

We love this soup on cold or rainy days.
It is creamy, hot, and delicious!

12 strips bacon, cut up
2 cups cubed potatoes
1 cup water
½ teaspoon salt
¼ teaspoon Shipshewana
　Happy Salt or seasoned salt
½ teaspoon onion powder

Pepper to taste
1 can cream of chicken soup
1 cup sour cream
1¾ cups milk
1 tablespoon parsley
Velveeta cheese to taste

In a 3-quart kettle, fry bacon until crisp. Pour off fat. Add potatoes, water, salt, Happy Salt, onion powder, and pepper. Bring to a boil. Cover and simmer for 10 to 15 minutes or until tender. Gradually stir in soup, sour cream, milk, parsley, and cheese. Heat, but do not boil. Serve hot.

NELSON AND JOANN MILLER FAMILY, Fredericktown, OH

Hearty Ham and Potato Soup

1 cup diced potatoes
1 cup diced carrots
½ cup chopped onion
½ cup chopped celery

2 cups chopped ham
1 quart milk
¼ cup butter
1 tablespoon flour

In a soup pot, cook potatoes, carrots, onion, celery, and ham in a little water until soft. Add milk and butter and bring to a boil. Mix flour with a little water and add to soup to thicken.

ANNA FISHER, Coatesville, PA

Beans and Corn Bread

1 tablespoon butter
2 tablespoons diced celery
1 teaspoon minced onion flakes
1 quart canned navy beans
1 cup diced ham
¼ teaspoon seasoned salt

Celery leaves
Dash garlic powder
Pepper
Pinch red pepper flakes
2 cups water

In a saucepan, sauté celery in butter. Add onion flakes when celery is translucent. Add beans, ham, and seasoned salt. Season to taste with celery leaves, garlic powder, pepper, and red pepper flakes. Add water and simmer 30 minutes. Serve with corn bread.

JUDITH MILLER, Fredericktown, OH

Taste of Home Tomato Soup

1 cup chopped celery
1 cup chopped onion
1 carrot, shredded
1 small green pepper, chopped
¼ cup butter or margarine
4½ cups chicken broth, divided

4 cups peeled and
  chopped tomatoes
2 teaspoons sugar
½ teaspoon curry powder
½ teaspoon salt
¼ teaspoon pepper
½ cup flour

In a 3-quart saucepan, cook celery, onion, carrot, and green pepper in butter until tender. Add 4 cups broth, tomatoes, sugar, curry powder, salt, and pepper. Bring to a boil. Reduce heat; simmer, uncovered, for 20 minutes. In a small bowl, stir flour and remaining ½ cup broth until smooth. Gradually stir into tomato mixture. Bring to a boil. Cook and stir until thick and bubbly, about 2 minutes.

NANCY ANN STOLTZFUS, Gap, PA

Family Favorite Rivel Soup

My whole family of twelve just loved Rivel Soup. I remember when I was a young scholar and fell asleep before supper. It didn't take long to come awake when it was said, "We have Rivel Soup."

1 pound ground beef
Onion, chopped
6 to 8 cups milk

2 eggs
½ to 1 teaspoon salt
2 cups flour

In a skillet, fry ground beef and onion to your taste. In a large saucepan, heat milk to boiling point. In a bowl, beat eggs and salt with a fork then cut in flour slowly to make crumbs (rivels). Sprinkle crumbs into boiling milk, stirring slowly so they don't clump. Add beef and onion and let soup boil until thickened.

EMMA GINGERICH, Bremen, OH

Rivel Soup

1 cup flour
¼ teaspoon salt

1 egg
3 to 4 cups meat broth

Place flour and salt in a bowl and make a well in center of flour. Place egg in well and work flour into egg with your fingers to make small crumbles. In a saucepan, bring broth to a boil. Sprinkle crumbs into broth, stirring as you add them. Simmer about 20 minutes. Variation: add finely diced potato to broth as it comes to a boil.

MRS. MELVIN (BERTHA) SCHWARTZ, Fredericktown, OH

PIONEER STEW

2 cups kidney beans
2 pounds ground beef
1 cup chopped onion
4 cups corn
4 cups green beans or peas

4 cups tomato juice
2 teaspoons salt
½ teaspoon chili powder
4 cups cooked macaroni
1 to 2 cups shredded cheese

Soak kidney beans overnight in water, then cook until softened. In a skillet, fry beef with onion. Add to beans. Add corn, green beans, tomato juice, salt, chili powder, and macaroni. Place in a roasting pan. Bake at 250 degrees for 2 to 3 hours. Top with cheese for the last 30 minutes.

Mrs. Menno J. Miller, Gallipolis, OH

PIZZA SOUP

1 pound sausage
¼ cup water
½ onion, chopped
½ green pepper, chopped
Italian seasoning, garlic
    powder, basil, rosemary,
    salt, and pepper to taste

2 quarts pizza sauce
4 cups water
2 ounces pepperoni, chopped
½ cup shredded
    mozzarella cheese

In a skillet, brown sausage. Add ¼ cup water, onion, and pepper, and sauté with sausage until tender. Add seasonings to taste. Put pizza sauce and 4 cups water in a large saucepan. Add sausage mixture and pepperoni. Bring to a boil and simmer for 15 minutes. When serving, top each bowl of soup with shredded mozzarella. This is very good with buttery corn bread.

Sharon Knepp, Chouteau, OK

Italian Soup

1 pound ground beef
1 cup chopped onion
1 quart spaghetti sauce
2 cups beef broth
1 cup chopped celery

1 teaspoon salt
½ teaspoon pepper
2 cups diced tomatoes
2 cups mixed vegetables

In a kettle, brown beef with onion and drain fat. Add spaghetti sauce, beef broth, celery, salt, and pepper. Simmer 20 minutes. Add tomatoes and vegetables; simmer 15 minutes more.

ANNA A. SLABAUGH, Apple Creek, OH

Chili Soup

1 pound ground beef
1 medium onion, chopped
2 teaspoons mustard
½ cup brown sugar
Salt and pepper to taste

1 scant tablespoon chili powder
2 cups tomato juice
2 cans kidney beans,
    drained and rinsed

In a large saucepan, brown beef. Add remaining ingredients and simmer for 1 hour.

Anna King, New Castle, IN

HEARTY HAMBURGER SOUP

1 pound ground beef
1 cup chopped onion
1 cup chopped green pepper
1 cup sliced carrots
1 cup diced potatoes

3 cups tomato juice
1½ teaspoons salt
½ teaspoon pepper
1 teaspoon chili powder
1 teaspoon Italian seasoning

In a large pot, fry beef; add onion and green pepper. Fry a couple more minutes. Add carrots, potatoes, tomato juice, salt, pepper, chili powder, and Italian seasoning. Cover and cook until vegetables are tender.

MOSES RIEHL, Coatsville, PA

CHEESEBURGER RICE SOUP

A very cozy and comforting soup for when the flu has come around.

1 cup chopped carrots
1 cup chopped celery
2 tablespoons butter
4 cups milk
4 teaspoons chicken seasoning
¼ teaspoon onion powder

1 pound Velveeta cheese
2 pounds ground beef or
  sausage, fried and crumbled
4 cups cooked rice
16 ounces sour cream
Salt and pepper to taste

In a stockpot, sauté carrots and celery in butter until tender. Add milk, chicken seasoning, onion powder, cheese, beef, and rice. Heat until hot throughout and cheese is melted. Remove from heat and add sour cream. Add salt and pepper to taste.

NELSON AND JOANN MILLER FAMILY, Fredericktown, OH

Chicken Rice Soup to Can

Having this canned soup on hand is much appreciated by mothers of sick children who aren't feeling well themselves.

¾ cup cooked chicken
⅓ cup brown rice
1 teaspoon salt
Dash pepper

⅓ cup diced celery
⅓ cup chopped carrots
1 tablespoon chopped onion
Chicken broth

In a quart jar, layer chicken, rice, salt, pepper, celery, carrot, and onion. Fill jar with broth (or chicken bouillon and water). Cold pack for 2½ hours.

Mrs. Reuben (Anna) Lapp, Rockville, IN

Williamsburg Inn Turkey Soup

A cozy, comforting soup from my mom's childhood days.

3 quarts turkey or chicken
  stock, divided
3 stalks celery, finely chopped
1 to 2 onions, finely chopped
2 large carrots, finely chopped
¼ cup long grain rice
1 cup finely diced
  potatoes (optional)

1 handful thin egg
  noodles (optional)
1 cup butter
1¼ cups flour
1 pint half-and-half
3 cups diced cooked turkey
½ teaspoon poultry seasoning
Salt and pepper to taste

In a saucepan, place 1 quart stock, celery, onions, carrots, rice, potatoes, and noodles. Cook for 20 minutes. Set aside. In a large soup kettle, melt butter. Blend in flour and heat until bubbly. Add half-and-half and remaining 2 quarts stock. Cook and stir until bubbly. Stir in reserved vegetables, turkey, poultry seasoning, salt, and pepper. Heat slowly to serving temperature.

Ioana Petersheim, Fredericktown, OH

Chicken Rice Soup

Here is a recipe that tastes very soothing when
sick with sore throat, head cold, flu, etc.

½ cup diced onion
¼ cup diced carrots
1 cup diced celery
2 tablespoons butter
1 quart chicken broth

2 quarts water
1 cup rice (I use white)
1 teaspoon chicken seasoning
Salt and pepper to taste

In a large saucepan, sauté vegetables in butter. Add broth and water; bring to a boil. Add rice, seasoning, salt, and pepper and return to a boil. Cover and let simmer for 30 minutes. Very delicious, especially served with bread, butter, and apple butter.

Mrs. John Lloyd Yoder, Newaygo, MI

PRESCRIPTION

5 drops of good manners
1 ounce common sense
1 ounce consideration

1 ounce good behavior
1 drop self-respect

Mix and shake well. Take 3 times a day.

ANNA A. SLABAUGH, Apple Creek, OH

INDULGENT DESSERTS

A home should be clean enough to be healthy, but dirty enough to be happy.

AMISH SAYING

Hot Caramel Apple Dip

½ cup butter   1 cup brown sugar
½ cup corn syrup   1 can sweetened condensed milk

In a saucepan, combine all ingredients and bring to a boil. Serve warm with slices of apples.

Malinda Gingerich, Spartansburg, PA

Hot Vanilla Pudding

This seems to be a comfort food for our family. As a girl I always loved hot pudding. Mom would make it for Sunday evening supper, and now I often do the same as my husband and children will ask for it. I still love mine hot, though my family prefers it after it cools a bit.

1 gallon milk
2 cups sifted flour
1½ cups sugar
8 eggs

Milk
¾ cup brown sugar
½ teaspoon salt
1 teaspoon vanilla

In a large pot, heat 1 gallon milk to boiling point. In a bowl, mix flour, sugar, and eggs; beat well. Add a bit of milk if needed to make a smooth mixture. Mix into boiling milk, stirring well. After it has come to a boil again for a few minutes, remove from heat and add brown sugar, salt, and vanilla. Serve hot with cookies, cake, crisp rice cereal mixed in, or just plain.

Note: If there are leftovers, use to make graham cracker pudding the next day by layering cracker crumbs between layers of pudding. Top with whipped topping. Chill at least 2 hours before serving.

MARY MILLER, Junction City, OH

Vanilla Pudding

My dear mother always made vanilla pudding every Saturday in case we got company on Sunday.

2 quarts milk
4 eggs
1¼ cups brown sugar

3 heaping tablespoons
cornstarch
Pinch salt
½ cup milk

In a saucepan, heat 2 quarts milk. In a bowl, beat eggs then add sugar and beat well. Stir in cornstarch and salt. Add ½ cup milk and mix well. Stir into hot milk in the saucepan. Stir until thickened. Cool. You may add whipped topping when serving if you wish.

SALOMIE E. GLICK, Howard, PA

CORNSTARCH PUDDING

1 quart milk
2 tablespoons cornstarch
1 tablespoon flour
2 eggs, beaten

1 cup sugar
2 teaspoons vanilla
½ teaspoon salt
Butter

In a saucepan, heat milk to boiling point. Combine cornstarch, flour, and eggs. Stir a small amount of the hot milk into mixture. Slowly add mixture to milk in saucepan. Add sugar. Cook and stir until thickened. Add vanilla and salt. Add butter to taste. Cool. My grandmother sometimes put crushed graham crackers and shredded coconut in her cooled pudding. You can also mix melted butter, brown sugar, and graham cracker crumbs together and layer with pudding in bowl(s). Top with whipped cream.

MARY ANN L. BYLER, New Wilmington, PA

CHOCOLATE PUDDING

6 tablespoons cocoa powder
1 cup sugar
6 tablespoons cornstarch
1 teaspoon salt

4 cups milk
4 egg yolks, beaten
2 teaspoons vanilla

In a bowl, mix cocoa powder, sugar, cornstarch, and salt. In a saucepan, combine milk and egg yolks, heating slowly. Add dry mixture, stirring often, cooking until thickened. Use alone for dessert or in making a pie.

MRS. JAMES MILLER, Guthrie, KY

FUDGE PUDDING QUICKIE

My mom made this often for dessert.

1 cup flour
¾ cup sugar
¼ teaspoon salt
2 teaspoons baking powder
2 tablespoons cocoa powder
2 tablespoons melted shortening

½ cup milk
½ cup chopped nuts
½ cup sugar
½ cup brown sugar
¼ cup cocoa powder

In a bowl, mix flour, ¾ cup sugar, salt, baking powder, 2 tablespoons cocoa powder, shortening, and milk until smooth. Mix in nuts. Pour into a greased 9x9-inch pan (larger is also okay). In a bowl, mix ½ cup sugar, brown sugar, and ¼ cup cocoa together and sprinkle over batter. Pour boiling water over all. Bake at 350 degrees for 30 to 55 minutes. Serve warm with ice cream, or cool and serve with whipped cream.

MARY ANN L. BYLER, New Wilmington, PA

EGG CUSTARD

12 egg yolks
3 whole eggs
2 quarts milk, heated to scald
½ cup sugar

⅓ cup maple syrup
Pinch salt
1 teaspoon vanilla
Cinnamon

Mix yolks, eggs, milk, sugar, maple syrup, salt, and vanilla well. Divide into half-pint jars (approximately 12 jars). Sprinkle with cinnamon. Place in a pan filled with ½ inch of water. Bake at 350 degrees for 50 minutes.

SADIE FISHER, Aaronsburg, PA

Butterscotch Tapioca

¼ cup butter
2 cups brown sugar
6 cups boiling water
1 teaspoon salt
1 cup pearl tapioca
2 eggs, beaten
½ cup sugar

1 cup milk
1 teaspoon vanilla
1 cup heavy cream, whipped,
  or 8 ounces whipped topping
4 Milky Way candy
  bars, chopped

In a saucepan, brown butter. Add brown sugar, boiling water, salt, and tapioca. Cook until tapioca is done. In a bowl, mix eggs with sugar and milk. Add to tapioca and cook until bubbly. Add vanilla. Cool. Fold in whipped cream and candy. Chill.

MARY N. SWARTZENTRUBER, Polk, OH

Orange Pineapple Tapioca

10 cups boiling water
1½ cups pearl tapioca
1 cup sugar
1 cup orange gelatin

2 (20 ounce) cans pineapple
  chunks, drained
Whipped topping

Into pot of boiling water, add tapioca and boil for 15 minutes. Set off heat until tapioca is clear and slightly cooled. Add sugar and gelatin. Mix well. Add pineapple. Chill. Before serving, mix in some whipped topping.

MENNO J. YODERS, Berlin, PA

MILK TAPIOCA

*My grandmother used to serve this with milk and fruit
when cooled. Brings back precious memories.*

2 quarts milk
¾ cup minute tapioca
3 eggs, beaten
1½ cups sugar

1 cup milk
1 tablespoon vanilla
½ teaspoon salt

In a saucepan, bring 2 quarts milk to a boil. Add tapioca and stir until tapioca is clear. In a bowl, mix eggs and sugar, then 1 cup milk. Quickly stir into tapioca. Cook until thick. Remove from heat and add vanilla and salt. Cool.

MARY ANN L. BYLER, New Wilmington, PA

Graham Cracker Fluff

4 tablespoons plain gelatin
1⅓ cups cold water
2 cups sugar
8 cups whole milk

2 eggs, separated
2 teaspoons vanilla
2 cups whipped cream

Soak gelatin in cold water. In a saucepan, combine sugar, milk, and egg yolks. Cook for 1 minute, stirring constantly. Remove from heat and add gelatin and vanilla. Chill until mixture begins to thicken. In a clean bowl, beat egg whites until stiff. Add to chilled mixture. Mix in whipped cream. Put in a dish lined with graham crackers. Sprinkle crushed graham crackers on top.

FANNIE L. STUTZMAN, West Salem, OH

Graham Pudding

My mother used to make this for supper approximately two times each winter when I was a young girl. I haven't had it for a long time, but it's a family favorite.

1 teaspoon baking soda
½ cup molasses
1 cup milk
½ cup sugar
½ teaspoon salt

1 teaspoon cinnamon
1 teaspoon baking powder
½ cup raisins
2 cups graham flour

In a mixing bowl, beat baking soda into molasses. Add milk, sugar, salt, cinnamon, and baking powder. Mix well. Stir in raisins. Add flour a bit at a time, stirring after each addition. Dough will be very stiff. Spray or grease a Bundt cake pan (not a pan that is 2 pieces) and spread dough into it evenly. Cover pan with a double layer of parchment or waxed paper and use masking or freezer tape to secure it tightly to outside of pan. Cover with a layer of aluminum foil and hold in place with rubber band or string to tightly seal pan. Place pan in a large pot and add hot water halfway up base of pan. (You don't want foil or paper touching the water.) Cover pot and bring water to a boil over medium heat. After it comes to a boil, lower heat to maintain a simmer. Steam the pudding for 2½ hours or until a cake tester comes out clean. Immediately turn pudding out onto a wire rack to cool.

Mrs. Moses Swartz, Mount Ayr, IA

DATE PUDDING

CAKE:

1 cup dates, finely chopped
1 teaspoon baking soda
1 cup hot water
1 cup brown sugar

1 tablespoon butter
1 cup flour
1 egg
½ cup nuts

Mix dates, baking soda, and water and let sit until cool. Add brown sugar, butter, flour, egg, and nuts. Stir. Preheat oven to 350 degrees. Pour into a greased baking pan. Bake 20 to 30 minutes.

SAUCE:

2 tablespoons butter
1 cup brown sugar
1½ cups water
3 tablespoons ClearJel
  or 2 tablespoons
  regular cornstarch
2 teaspoons vanilla

1½ teaspoons maple flavoring
2 tablespoons maple
  pancake syrup
Layers:
1 (8 ounce) carton frozen
  whipped topping, thawed
2 to 3 bananas, sliced

Boil butter, brown sugar, water, and ClearJel (cornstarch) for 10 minutes. Add vanilla, maple flavoring, and syrup. When ready to serve, alternate layers of cake, sauce, whipped topping, and bananas.

MRS. HARVEY R. MILLER, South Dayton, NY

Bread Pudding

1 loaf homemade bread
2 cups heavy cream
2 cups milk
3 large eggs, beaten

2 cups sugar
1 teaspoon vanilla
1½ teaspoons cinnamon
¼ cup butter, melted

Tear bread into small pieces and place in a large bowl. Add cream and milk. Let stand 10 minutes. Stir mixture well. Add eggs, sugar, vanilla, and cinnamon. Stir well. Pour butter into a 9x13-inch pan. Spoon pudding mixture into pan. Bake uncovered at 325 degrees for 55 to 60 minutes.

Sauce:

½ cup butter
1 cup sugar

⅔ cup heavy cream

In a saucepan, cook butter, sugar, and cream until sugar dissolves. Simmer 5 minutes. Drizzle over pudding.

Emmie Schwartz, Berne, IN

Yummy Jello

2½ cups boiling water
12 ounces flavored gelatin

3 ounces vanilla instant
pudding mix
1 cup milk

Mix gelatin in boiling water. Let cool awhile. In another bowl, beat pudding mix and milk for 2 minutes. Mix into gelatin and pour into a 9x13-inch pan. Refrigerate until firm.

Mrs. Reuben (Anna) Lapp, Rockville, IN

Chocolate Heath Bar Dessert

4 cups cubed chocolate
angel food cake
2 cups chocolate pudding

⅓ cup crushed toffee candy bar
1 (8 ounce) carton
whipped topping

Layer half of the cake in a trifle bowl. Top with half of the pudding, half of the candy, and half of the whipped topping. Repeat layers. Decorate with additional candy if desired. Chill several hours.

Mrs. James Miller, Guthrie, KY

Pineapple Dessert

2½ cups quick oats
1 cup flour
⅛ teaspoon baking soda
1 cup butter
1 (8 ounce) can crushed
pineapple

½ cup heavy cream
1 cup sugar
1 tablespoon cornstarch
1 cup whipped cream

In a mixing bowl, combine oats, flour, baking soda, and butter until crumbly. Press into a 6x10-inch pan. To make filling, in a saucepan, mix pineapple, heavy cream, sugar, and cornstarch. Cook until thickened, stirring constantly. Pour over crust. Bake at 375 degrees for 30 minutes. Serve cold with whipped cream.

Mary N. Swartzentruber, Polk, OH

PEANUT BUTTER CUP DESSERT

CRUST:

½ cup margarine or
 butter, melted
1 cup sugar
1 egg
1 teaspoon vanilla

1¼ cups flour
½ cup cocoa powder
¾ teaspoon baking soda
¼ teaspoon salt

In a mixing bowl, cream together margarine, sugar, egg, and vanilla. Add flour, cocoa powder, baking soda, and salt. Mix well and press into a greased 9x13-inch pan. Bake at 350 degrees for 10 minutes. Do not overbake. Cool.

FILLING:

8 ounces cream cheese
¾ cup peanut butter
1 cup powdered sugar

16 ounces whipped
 topping, divided
Peanut butter cups, chopped
Caramel sauce (optional)

In a bowl, beat together cream cheese and peanut butter. Beat in powdered sugar. Mix in 8 ounces whipped topping. Spread over cooked crust. Top with 8 ounces whipped topping. Sprinkle with peanut butter cups. You can drizzle with caramel sauce if desired.

SUSAN L. YODER, Allensville, PA

BROWN SUGAR DUMPLINGS

*My grandmother used to make this with raisins
in it and I thought it was delicious.*

¾ cup milk
1 cup sugar
1 teaspoon butter
1½ teaspoons baking powder
2 cups flour
1 cup raisins, nuts, or dates

½ teaspoon salt
2 cups water
2 cups brown sugar
1 tablespoon butter
Dash vanilla

Mix together milk, sugar, 1 teaspoon butter, baking powder, flour, raisins, and salt; set aside. In a saucepan, combine water, brown sugar, 1 tablespoon butter, and vanilla and bring to a boil. Carefully pour into a 9x13-inch pan. Drop dough by spoonfuls onto syrup. Bake at 350 degrees for 30 to 40 minutes. Serve with whipped cream.

MARY ANN L. BYLER, New Wilmington, PA

CARAMEL DUMPLINGS

SAUCE:

2 tablespoons butter
1½ cups packed brown sugar

1½ cups water

In a skillet, heat butter, brown sugar, and water to boiling. Reduce heat to simmer.

DUMPLINGS:

1¼ cups flour
½ cup sugar
1 teaspoon baking powder
½ teaspoon salt

½ cup milk
2 tablespoons butter
1 teaspoon vanilla

Mix all ingredients in a bowl. Drop by tablespoonfuls into simmering sauce. Cover skillet tightly and simmer for 20 minutes. Do not lift lid. Serve warm with ice cream.

DAVID BYLER, New Castle, PA

APPLE ROLL-UPS

PASTRY:

2 cups flour	⅔ cup shortening
2½ teaspoons baking powder	⅔ cup milk
½ teaspoon salt	

In a bowl, sift flour, baking powder, and salt together. Cut in shortening until crumbles are about the size of small peas. Sprinkle in milk and lightly press together dough only until it is just holding together. Roll pastry into 1 large rectangular sheet that is ¼ inch thick.

FILLING:

4 tablespoons melted butter	1 teaspoon cinnamon
½ cup brown sugar	6 baking apples, chopped

In a bowl, combine melted butter, brown sugar, and cinnamon. Spread mixture over pastry. Sprinkle with chopped apples. Roll pastry up like a jelly roll. Cut 1¼-inch slices. Place slices in a greased 9x13-inch pan.

SAUCE:

2 cups brown sugar	¼ teaspoon cinnamon
2 cups water	¼ teaspoon nutmeg
¼ cup butter	

In a saucepan over low heat, cook together brown sugar, water, butter, cinnamon, and nutmeg for 10 minutes. Pour sauce over pastry slices. Bake at 375 degrees for 35 to 40 minutes. Serve warm with whipped cream or milk. Serves 8.

ANITA PETERSHEIM, Fredericktown, OH

Honey Baked Apples

6 medium baking apples
1½ tablespoons melted butter
¼ cup honey

¾ cup whole-grain cereal
(e.g. Grape Nuts)
¼ cup raisins

Wash and core apples. Peel half the apple or slit peel horizontally around each apple about 1 inch from top to allow steam to escape. Place apples in a baking dish lined with aluminum foil. Bake at 400 degrees for 40 minutes. In a bowl, combine butter, honey, cereal, and raisins. Fill apples with mixture and bake an additional 10 minutes.

Betty Marcak, Shiner, TX

Apple Fritters

1 cup flour
½ teaspoon salt
½ teaspoon baking powder
¾ cup hot milk
1 egg

4 to 5 apples
Fat or oil for frying
Brown sugar
Apple butter
Maple syrup

In a bowl, sift together flour, salt, and baking powder. In another bowl, mix hot milk and egg. Add flour and beat to a smooth batter. Peel, core, and slice apples into rings. Dip rings in batter and fry in hot fat or oil until a nice golden brown. Remove from oil and drain on paper towels. Sprinkle with brown sugar. Eat while hot with apple butter or maple syrup.

Mrs. Melvin (Bertha) Schwartz, Fredericktown, OH

Apple Torte

This is one of my mom's desserts.

1 cup peeled and chopped apples
1 cup chopped nuts
1 cup flour
1 cup sugar
1 egg, beaten

½ teaspoon salt
1 teaspoon baking soda
1 teaspoon vanilla
3 tablespoons melted butter

In a bowl, mix all ingredients well. Spread in a greased 9x9-inch pan. Bake at 350 degrees for 30 minutes or until it tests done. Serve with whipped cream.

Mary Ann L. Byler, New Wilmington, PA

Fresh Apple Cake

1½ cups canola oil
2 cups sugar
1 teaspoon vanilla
3 cups chopped apples
2 eggs
2½ cups flour

1 teaspoon baking soda
1 teaspoon baking powder
½ teaspoon salt
1 teaspoon cinnamon
1 teaspoon nutmeg
1 cup chopped nuts

In a mixing bowl, combine oil, sugar, vanilla, and apples. Blend in eggs. In another bowl, combine flour, baking soda, baking powder, salt, cinnamon, and nutmeg. Add to first mixture. Stir in nuts. Pour into a greased 9x13-inch pan and bake at 350 degrees for 45 minutes or until it tests done with a toothpick.

Aaron (Emma) Gingerich, Bremen, OH

TEA CAKES

½ cup butter, softened
1 cup sugar
2 eggs, beaten
1 teaspoon milk
1 teaspoon vanilla
1 teaspoon lemon extract

2½ cups flour
1 teaspoon baking powder
1 teaspoon baking soda
½ teaspoon salt
1 teaspoon nutmeg

In a mixing bowl, cream butter and sugar. Add eggs, milk, vanilla, and lemon extract; beat well. In another bowl, combine flour, baking powder, baking soda, salt, and nutmeg. Add to creamed mixture, mixing well. On a lightly floured surface, roll dough out to ¼-inch thickness. Cut dough with a 2-inch round cookie cutter. Place on an ungreased cookie sheet. Bake at 350 degrees for 10 to 12 minutes or until lightly browned. Yields 4 dozen.

JUDITH MILLER, Fredericktown, OH

GRAND CHAMPION SPONGE CAKE

We always had this for our birthday cake.

6 egg whites
1 teaspoon cream of tartar
½ cup sugar
6 egg yolks
¼ cup water

1 teaspoon vanilla
1¼ cups flour
1 cup sugar
½ teaspoon baking powder
½ teaspoon baking soda

In a large bowl, beat egg whites until frothy. Add cream of tartar. Gradually add sugar, beating until stiff. In a small mixing bowl, combine egg yolks, water, and vanilla. Beat. Add flour, sugar, baking powder, and baking soda. Mix in egg whites gently. Place in an ungreased 10-inch tube pan. Bake at 300 to 350 degrees for 45 minutes. Invert pan to cool. Frost as desired.

MENNO J. YODERS, Berlin, PA

Banana Cake

3⅓ cups flour
¾ teaspoon baking soda
3¾ teaspoon baking powder
¾ teaspoon salt
¾ cup butter, softened

3 eggs
1½ cups sugar
1 teaspoon vanilla
⅓ cup sour milk
1½ cups mashed ripe bananas

In a mixing bowl, combine flour, baking soda, baking powder, and salt. In another bowl, mix butter, eggs, sugar, and vanilla. Add wet mixture to dry mixture alternately with milk and bananas. Place in a greased and floured 9x13-inch pan. Bake at 350 degrees for 25 to 30 minutes or until it tests done. Good frosted with a cream cheese frosting. You can also combine mashed banana, softened butter, and powdered sugar to make a frosting.

ESTHER L. MILLER, Fredericktown, OH

Swiss Roll Cake

2 cups flour
1½ cups sugar
½ cup cocoa powder
2 teaspoons baking powder
1 teaspoon baking soda

½ teaspoon salt
2 eggs
1 cup butter, melted
1 cup hot water
1 cup milk

Combine flour, sugar, cocoa, baking powder, baking soda, and salt. Stir in eggs and melted butter. Add hot water and milk. Stir until combined. Pour into a well-greased and floured 12x17-inch pan. Bake at 350 degrees for 30 minutes or until an inserted toothpick comes out clean. Cool slightly, then turn out onto a clean dish towel dusted with powdered sugar. Roll cake starting from shortest end. Cool completely.

FILLING:

1 (8 ounce) package cream
  cheese, softened
½ cup powdered sugar

1 (16 ounce) tub
  whipped topping

Beat together cream cheese and powdered sugar until light and fluffy. Fold in whipped topping. Unroll cake and spread with filling. Reroll cake.

FROSTING:

5 tablespoons butter

1½ cups chocolate chips

In a saucepan, melt butter gently. Remove from heat and add chocolate chips, stirring until melted and smooth. Pour over cake roll. Chill.

Mrs. Elizabeth Yoder, Barnsville, OH

Chocolate Angel Food Cake

2 cups egg whites
2 cups sugar, divided
1½ teaspoons cream of tartar
1 teaspoon vanilla

¾ cup cake flour
¾ cup cocoa powder
1 teaspoon salt

Beat egg whites until soft peaks form. Add 1 cup sugar and cream of tartar; beat until stiff. Beat in vanilla. Sift together flour, cocoa powder, salt, and 1 cup sugar. Fold gently into egg whites with a wire whisk, adding only ⅓ of dry mixture at a time. Pour into a tube pan and bake at 325 degrees for 15 minutes. Raise temperature to 350 degrees for 40 minutes or until done. Turn pan upside down when removed from oven to cool.

Mrs. James Miller, Guthrie, KY

Chocolate Mayonnaise Cake

A favorite family chocolate cake.

3 cups flour
1½ cups sugar
2 teaspoons baking soda
2 teaspoons baking powder

6 tablespoons cocoa powder
1 cup mayonnaise
2 cups water

Sift together flour, sugar, baking soda, baking powder, and cocoa powder. Mix in mayonnaise and water until well combined. Place in a greased and floured 9x13-inch pan. Bake at 350 degrees for 40 minutes.

Mrs. Daniel Stoltzfus, Nottingham, PA

Magic Salted Caramel Cupcakes

(Gluten free)

2 (15 ounce) cans white
   beans, rinsed
3 large eggs
¾ cup egg whites
¾ to 1 cup sugar or Gentle
   Sweet sugar substitute

2 teaspoons baking powder
1 teaspoon baking soda
1 teaspoon vanilla
1 teaspoon caramel extract
¼ teaspoon salt
2 tablespoons coconut oil

In a blender, place beans, eggs, egg whites, sugar, baking powder, baking soda, vanilla, caramel extract, salt, and coconut oil and blend well. Spray cupcake liners with cooking spray before filling with batter. Bake at 350 degrees for 25 minutes. Cool and refrigerate for 4 to 6 hours before serving to reduce bean flavor. Frost, then drizzle with caramel sauce.

Frosting:

3 ounces cream cheese
½ cup heavy cream
¼ cup sugar or Gentle
   Sweet sugar substitute

¼ teaspoon caramel extract
½ teaspoon vanilla
5 pinches salt

Blend all ingredients in a blender until smooth and somewhat thickened.

Caramel sauce:

2 tablespoons butter
2 tablespoons sugar or Gentle
   Sweet sugar substitute
½ teaspoon molasses

2 tablespoons cream
⅛ teaspoon salt
⅛ teaspoon xanthan gum

In a saucepan, melt together butter, sugar, and molasses, stirring constantly. Add cream and salt. Stir in xanthan gum and allow to cool to thicken.

Glenda Schwartz, Milford, IN

CHOCOLATE CHIP TARTS

1 cup butter
¼ cup sugar
¾ cup brown sugar
2 eggs
1 teaspoon vanilla
1 teaspoon baking soda
½ cup vanilla instant
   pudding mix

2¼ cups flour
2½ cups mini chocolate chips
8 ounces cream cheese
½ cup powdered sugar
2 cups whipped topping
Additional chocolate
   chips for decorating

In a mixing bowl, cream butter, sugar, and brown sugar. Add eggs and vanilla; beat well. Add baking soda and pudding mix then add flour. Stir in chocolate chips. Put in a well-greased tart pan and bake at 350 degrees for 8 to 10 minutes. After removing from oven, press center using a bottle cap. Cool. In a bowl, blend cream cheese, powdered sugar, and whipped topping. Divide into center of tarts. Sprinkle with chocolate chips. Chill.

EMMA ESH, Gordonville, PA

FRUIT CAKE DESSERT

1 chocolate cake or brownie mix
1 (8 ounce) package cream
   cheese, softened
1½ cups powdered sugar
1 (8 ounce) carton
   whipped topping

Fresh fruit
½ cup butter or margarine
2 cups semisweet
   chocolate chips

Mix cake mix according to directions. Divide into 2 greased 9x9-inch pans and bake according to directions. Cool. In a mixing bowl, beat together cream cheese, powdered sugar, and whipped topping. Spread over 1 9x9-inch cake. Top with fresh fruit of choice. Combine butter and chocolate chips and melt together over low heat or in a microwave. Drizzle over fruit. (You will have one cake leftover to use as you wish.)

EMMA ESH, Gordonville, PA

Cinnamon Flop

My mother often made Cinnamon Flop. It is so simple and good.

½ cup sugar
1 cup milk
2 cups flour
¼ cup butter

2 teaspoons baking powder
butter
cinnamon
sugar

Mix first 5 ingredients, stirring well. Place in an 8x11-inch pan and bake at 350 degrees for 30 minutes. While cake is still warm, spread with butter. Sprinkle with a mixture of cinnamon and sugar. Delicious served with strawberries and blueberries.

SADIE FISHER, Aaronsburg, PA

APPLE GOODIE

1½ cups sugar
2 tablespoons flour
Pinch salt
1 teaspoon cinnamon
6 cups sliced apples
1 cup oats

1 cup brown sugar
1 cup flour
¼ teaspoon baking soda
⅓ teaspoon baking powder
⅔ cup butter

In a bowl, mix sugar, 2 tablespoons flour, salt, and cinnamon. Add apples and stir to coat. Put in a greased 9x13-inch pan or roaster. In another bowl, mix oats, brown sugar, 1 cup flour, baking soda, and baking powder. Cut in butter until mixture is crumbly. Put on top of apples. Pat down firmly. Bake at 350 degrees for 35 to 40 minutes until brown and crust has formed. Serve with milk or cream.

SUSIE SCHLABACH, Spencer, OH

Apple Rhubarb Oatmeal Crunch

3 cups sliced apples
1 cup chopped fresh rhubarb
¾ cup sugar
1 tablespoon flour
½ teaspoon cinnamon

¾ cup oats
¼ cup flour
¼ cup brown sugar
¼ cup butter

In a mixing bowl, combine apples, rhubarb, sugar, 1 tablespoon flour, and cinnamon. Put in a greased baking dish. In another bowl, mix oats, ¼ cup flour, brown sugar, and butter until crumbly. Spread over apple mixture. Bake at 375 degrees for 35 to 40 minutes or until apples are soft and crust is lightly browned. Serve warm with milk.

Katie Gingerich, Dalton, OH

Rhubarb Crunch

3 cups chopped rhubarb
5 cups water
2 cups sugar
6 heaping tablespoons
 Therm Flo (cornstarch)

½ cup strawberry gelatin
2 cups flour
2 cups quick oats
2 cups brown sugar
1 cup butter, melted

In a saucepan, cook rhubarb in water and sugar until tender. In a small bowl, mix Therm Flo (cornstarch) with enough water to form a paste. While hot, mix in Thermo Flo and gelatin into rhubarb, stirring until thickened. Cool. In a bowl, mix flour, oats, brown sugar, and butter. Pat about half of mixture into a 9x13-inch pan to form a thin crust. Pour rhubarb on top. Sprinkle with remaining crumbs. Bake at 350 degrees for 30 minutes until golden brown. Very good served warm with vanilla ice cream.

Barbara Miller, Constable, NY

Rhubarb Torte

CRUST:

> 2 cups flour
> 2 tablespoons sugar

> 1 cup butter

Mix all ingredients and press into a 9x13-inch pan. Bake at 350 degrees for 10 to 15 minutes. Cool.

FILLING:

> 6 egg yolks, beaten
> 2 cups sugar
> ¼ cup flour

> ⅛ teaspoon salt
> 1 cup heavy cream
> 5 cups chopped rhubarb

Mix all ingredients together. Pour over cooled crust. Bake at 350 degrees for 50 to 60 minutes.

MERINGUE:

> 6 egg whites
> ⅛ teaspoon cream of tartar

> ¾ cup sugar

Beat egg whites and cream of tartar until soft peaks form. Gradually add sugar, beating until soft peaks form again. Pour over filling and bake at 350 degrees for 12 to 15 minutes or until lightly browned.

MALINDA GINGERICH, Spartansburg, PA

Raspberry Swirl Cheesecake

We use this recipe for weddings. Very delicious!

1¼ cups graham cracker crumbs
6 tablespoons butter, softened
2 tablespoons brown sugar
1 (8 ounce) package cream
   cheese, softened

1 (14 ounce) can condensed milk
¼ cup lemon juice
1 egg, beaten
1 cup raspberry pie filling

In a mixing bowl, combine cracker crumbs, butter, and brown sugar together and press into a springform pan or 9x13-inch pan. In another bowl, beat together cream cheese, condensed milk, lemon juice, and egg. Spread over cracker crust. Swirl pie filling on top. Bake at 400 degrees for 15 minutes. Let cool completely before adding the next filling.

Filling:

10 ounces cream
   cheese, softened
½ cup powdered sugar
1 teaspoon vanilla

½ teaspoon lemon juice
1 cup heavy whipping cream
1 cup crushed Oreo cookies
Fresh fruit

In a bowl, beat together cream cheese, powdered sugar, vanilla, and lemon juice until smooth. Add cream and cookies. Spread over baked cheesecake. Top with fresh fruit of choice (for example, pineapple, banana, grapes, oranges, or raspberries).

Glaze:

1 cup boiling water
2 tablespoons Therm
   Flo (cornstarch)

Pineapple gelatin

Mix boiling water and Therm Flo. Add gelatin to suit your taste. Drizzle over fruit and chill.

EDNA J. HERSHBERGER, North Lawrence, NY

FROZEN CHEESECAKE

2 cups graham cracker crumbs
½ cup sugar, divided
½ cup butter, melted
16 ounces cream
  cheese, softened

2 eggs, beaten
16 ounces whipped topping
Fruit pie filling

In a bowl, mix cracker crumbs, ¼ cup sugar, and butter. Press into a 9x13-inch pan. In another bowl, mix cream cheese and ¼ cup sugar. Add beaten eggs and whipped topping, mixing well. Spread onto crust and freeze. Top with your favorite fruit filling when ready to serve. Or, you can swirl the fruit filling into the cream cheese mixture before freezing.

MRS. JOSEPH MILLER, Navarre, OH

BLUEBERRY YOGURT PIE

2 (8 ounce) packages cream
  cheese, softened
1 can sweetened condensed milk
3 cups plain yogurt
2 tablespoons lemon juice
1 quart blueberry pie filling

1 (8 ounce) carton
  whipped topping
Fresh blueberries
3 (8 inch) graham
  cracker piecrusts

In a large bowl, beat cream cheese until fluffy. Gradually beat in condensed milk until smooth. Stir in yogurt and lemon juice. Fold in pie filling then whipped topping. Fold in some fresh blueberries if desired. Divide into 3 piecrusts. Garnish with fresh blueberries if desired. Chill.

IDA BONTRAGER, Kenton, OH

Chocolate Custard Pie

2 tablespoons flour
1½ cups sugar
2 tablespoons cocoa powder
Pinch salt
2 cups milk, scalded

2 teaspoons vanilla
2 eggs, separated
2 tablespoons butter
1 large unbaked piecrust

In a bowl, mix flour, sugar, cocoa powder, and salt. Mix into a saucepan of scalded milk removed from heat. Add vanilla, egg yolks, and butter. Mix well. Beat egg whites stiff and fold into milk mixture. Pour into unbaked piecrust. (This recipe doubled fills 3 small pie shells.) Bake at 400 degrees for 10 minutes. Reduce heat to 350 degrees and bake 25 to 30 minutes until a knife dipped into the middle comes out clean.

Mrs. Jacob Leanna Yoder, Patriot, OH

CARAMEL CHOCOLATE CREAM CHEESE PIE

1 can sweetened condensed milk
1 (8 ounce) package cream
  cheese, softened
1 (8 ounce) carton
  whipped topping

2 (9 inch) baked piecrusts
Caramel ice cream
  topping sauce
Chocolate ice cream
  topping sauce
Fresh fruit

In a bowl, mix condensed milk and cream cheese until smooth. Beat in whipped topping. Divide into 2 piecrusts. Swirl caramel and chocolate sauces over top. Top with fresh fruit of choice.

JERRY AND IDA PETERSHEIM, Kenton, OH

CHOCOLATE CREAM CHEESE PIE

1 to 1½ cups milk
  chocolate chips
⅔ cup milk, divided
1 (8 ounce) package cream
  cheese, softened

½ cup brown sugar
1 (16 ounce) carton
  whipped topping
2 (9 inch) baked piecrusts

In a saucepan, combine chocolate chips with ½ cup milk and melt over very low heat. Remove from heat. In a bowl, blend cream cheese and brown sugar, then stir into chocolate and add remaining milk. Fold in whipped topping. Divide into 2 baked piecrusts. Best if refrigerated for at least 12 hours. They will freeze well also.

IDA BONTRAGER, Kenton, OH

Paper Bag Apple Pie

Apples, peeled and sliced
½ cup sugar
1 tablespoon flour
1 unbaked piecrust
Cinnamon

2 tablespoons butter
6 tablespoons butter
¾ cup brown sugar
½ cup flour

Mix apples (enough to fill the piecrust) with sugar and 1 tablespoon flour. Dump into piecrust and sprinkle with cinnamon. Pat with 2 tablespoons butter. In a bowl, mix 6 tablespoons butter, brown sugar, and ½ cup flour. Put over apples. Slide into a heavy grocery paper bag and bake at 350 degrees for 1 hour. This works best in a gas oven. I never leave the house while I bake this pie because of the bag.

BARBARA COBLENTZ, Greenfield, OH

Ground Cherry Pie

Picking ground cherries can become a boring task for a child, but it can be worth it when Mother promises pies.

4 cups ground cherries
3 cups sugar, divided
4 cups heavy cream
4 cups milk

1½ cups Perma-Flo
1 small box cherry gelatin
1 small box orange gelatin
4 baked piecrusts

In a saucepan, cover cherries with water and add 1 cup sugar. Heat until cherries are partly cooked. In another saucepan, heat cream and milk to a boil, then add to cherries. In a bowl, combine Perma-Flo and 2 cups sugar with enough water to make a paste. Add to cherries and stir until it starts to thicken. Remove from heat and add cherry and orange gelatin. Divide cherry filling into 4 baked piecrusts.

EMMA GINGERICH, Bremen, OH

MOM'S CARAMEL PIE

This recipe comes from my deceased aunt. She knew how to make something good without expensive ingredients.

3 tablespoons butter
½ cup hot water
½ teaspoon baking soda
1½ cups brown sugar
2½ cups water
4 tablespoons flour

½ cup sugar
2 egg yolks
½ teaspoon salt
1 teaspoon vanilla
1 baked piecrust
2 egg whites

In a saucepan, combine butter and ½ cup hot water. Add baking soda and brown sugar and bring to a boil until mixture browns. Add 2½ cups water. In a bowl, blend flour, sugar, egg yolks, and salt until smooth. Add to saucepan mixture and bring to a boil, stirring until thickened. Remove from heat and add vanilla. Pour into baked piecrust. Beat egg whites to a stiff peak and spread over pie. Brown lightly under a broiler.

DAVID BYLER, New Castle, PA

Oatmeal Pie

This recipe comes from my mom. Just simple ingredients that make something so good!

3 eggs, beaten
⅔ cup sugar
1 cup brown sugar
2 teaspoons butter, softened
⅔ cup oats

⅔ cup milk
1 teaspoon vanilla
¾ teaspoon salt
1 unbaked piecrust

In a bowl, mix eggs, sugar, brown sugar, and butter. Add oats, milk, vanilla, and salt. Mix well. Pour into unbaked piecrust. Bake at 350 degrees for 30 to 35 minutes.

David Byler, New Castle, PA

Raisin Crumb Pie

¾ cup raisins
⅔ cup brown sugar
2 cups water, divided
2 tablespoons cornstarch
¾ tablespoon vinegar
Pinch salt

1 (9 inch) unbaked piecrust
1 scant cup flour
½ cup brown sugar
¼ cup butter
½ teaspoon baking soda

In a saucepan, bring raisins and ⅔ cup brown sugar to a boil in 1¾ cups water. In a small bowl, blend ¼ cup water and cornstarch into a paste. Add to raisins with vinegar and salt. Pour into piecrust. In a bowl, combine flour, ½ cup brown sugar, butter, and baking soda until crumbly. Put onto raisin filling. Bake at 375 degrees for 40 to 45 minutes.

Martha Beachy, Butler, OH

Delicious Mince Pies

I have good memories of my mother making these.

6 cups ground or minced beef
2 cups raisins
1½ cups sugar
2 cups brown sugar
2 lemons, whole and ground
2 quarts chopped apples
1 cup molasses

1 teaspoon ground cloves
2 teaspoons cinnamon
1 teaspoon nutmeg
½ cup vinegar
½ cup water
8 small unbaked piecrusts

Mix all ingredients well and divide into piecrusts. Bake at 350 degrees for 45 minutes. Serve warm.

Sadie Fisher, Aaronsburg, PA

Pecan Pie

3 eggs
2 tablespoons flour
½ cup sugar
2 tablespoons butter
¾ cup corn syrup

¾ cup water
½ teaspoon vanilla
Salt to taste
1 cup pecans
1 unbaked piecrust

Mix eggs, flour, sugar, butter, corn syrup, water, vanilla, and salt. Stir in pecans. Pour into unbaked piecrust.

Lovina Gingerich, Dalton, OH

RHUBARB PIE

This is a family favorite.

1 heaping cup chopped
 fresh rhubarb
1 cup sugar
2 eggs
¾ cup heavy cream
6 crackers, crushed (optional)

¼ teaspoon salt
2 teaspoons butter
Dash nutmeg
1 unbaked piecrust,
 plus dough for top

In a small bowl, combine rhubarb and sugar and let sit for at least 1 hour. In a mixing bowl, beat eggs. Add cream, crackers, salt, butter, and nutmeg. Mix in rhubarb. Pour mixture into unbaked crust. Cut strips of pie dough and ladder strips across the top. Seal edges.

VERNA D. GINGERICH, Mount Ayr, IA

MOTHER'S PUMPKIN PIE

This is one of my favorite pies. We always have it for Thanksgiving.

CRUST:

3 cups flour	½ cup water
1 tablespoon salt	1 teaspoon vinegar
1 cup lard	1 egg, beaten

In a mixing bowl, combine flour and salt, cutting in lard until mixture resembles coarse crumbs. Mix water and vinegar and add it with egg to crumbled mixture, stirring until it forms a ball, but do not overmix. It may need a bit more water. Separate dough into 3 parts and roll each out to line 3 pie pans.

FILLING:

6 eggs	3 tablespoons flour
1½ cups sugar	2 scant teaspoons salt
1½ cups brown sugar	2 teaspoons pumpkin pie spice
1 quart pumpkin puree	1 quart evaporated milk

In a bowl, beat eggs. Add sugar, brown sugar, pumpkin, flour, salt, and spice and beat until smooth. Stir in milk and beat well. Pour into unbaked piecrusts. Bake at 400 degrees for 5 to 10 minutes. Reduce heat to 350 degrees and bake for 20 to 30 minutes until almost set.

IDA BYLER, Frazeysburg, OH

MONTGOMERY PIE

This was my mother's recipe.

BASE:

½ cup molasses
¼ cup sugar
1 egg
1 cup water

2 tablespoons flour
½ lemon, juice and zest
1 (9 inch) unbaked piecrust

In a bowl, combine molasses, sugar, egg, water, flour, lemon juice, and lemon zest. Pour into unbaked piecrust.

TOPPING:

¼ cup sugar
¼ cup butter
1 egg, beaten

½ teaspoon baking soda
1¼ cups flour
½ cup sour milk

In a bowl, combine sugar and butter. Add beaten egg and beat thoroughly. In another bowl, sift baking soda and flour. Add to first mixture alternately with milk. Spread over base. Bake at 375 degrees for 35 to 40 minutes.

SADIE FISHER, Aaronsburg, PA

PEANUT BUTTER PIE

1 (8 ounce) package cream
   cheese, softened
1 cup powdered sugar
½ cup peanut butter

½ cup milk
1 (8 ounce) tub whipped topping
1 baked piecrust, Oreo
   crust, or graham crust

In a bowl, beat cream cheese until fluffy. Mix in sugar and peanut butter slowly. Add milk and mix well. Fold in whipped topping. Pour mixture into baked piecrust.

MARLENE STOLTZFUS, Gap, PA

Oreo Peanut Butter Pie

CRUST:

1¼ cups Oreo cookie crumbs   ¼ cup butter
¼ cup sugar

Mix all ingredients, divide, and press into 2 pie pans. Save some crumbs for topping.

FILLING:

8 ounces cream cheese   1 cup powdered sugar
1 cup peanut butter   8 ounces whipped topping
1 tablespoon butter   1 teaspoon vanilla

In a mixing bowl, beat together cream cheese, peanut butter, and butter. Add powdered sugar, whipped topping, and vanilla and beat until smooth. Divide and fill both piecrusts. Sprinkle with reserved crumbs. Chill.

AARON (EMMA) GINGERICH, Bremen, OH

FAVORITE BROWNIES

Great treat for family gatherings or church
carry-ins, or to freeze for later.

3 cups butter, softened
6 cups sugar (or less)
2 tablespoons vanilla
12 eggs
4¾ cups flour

2 cups cocoa powder
2 teaspoons baking powder
2 teaspoons salt
2 cups chocolate chips

In a large bowl, mix ingredients, except chocolate chips, in order given. Pour into 2 large greased jelly roll pans. Sprinkle 1 cup chocolate chips on each pan. Bake at 350 degrees for 40 minutes. Do not overbake.

ELIZABETH SHETLER, Brinkhaven, OH

BEST BLONDIE BROWNIES

(Gluten free)

¾ cup butter or coconut oil
¾ cup coconut sugar
¼ cup honey
4 eggs
2 teaspoons vanilla

2 cups almond flour
⅓ cup coconut flour
1 teaspoon baking soda
½ teaspoon salt
1 cup chocolate chips

In a mixing bowl, combine butter, sugar, and honey. Beat in eggs. Add vanilla. Mix in almond flour, coconut flour, baking soda, and salt. Fold in chocolate chips. Spread into a greased 9x13-inch pan. Bake at 350 degrees for 20 to 25 minutes.

LINDA BEILER, Gordonville, PA

CAN'T-LEAVE-ALONE BARS

1 box white or chocolate
   cake mix
2 eggs
⅓ cup oil

¼ cup butter
1 cup chocolate chips
1 can sweetened condensed milk

In a bowl, mix cake mix, eggs, and oil using a fork. Reserve ¾ cup crumbs. Press remaining mixture in bottom of a 9x13-inch pan. Melt butter, chocolate chips, and sweetened condensed milk together and pour over crust. Top with reserved crumbs. Bake at 350 degrees for 20 to 30 minutes or until browned on top.

IOANA PETERSHEIM, Fredericktown, OH

CHOCOLATE BARS

1 cup butter, melted
1½ cups sugar
4 eggs
4 tablespoons cocoa powder
1½ cups flour

½ teaspoon baking powder
Pinch salt
2 teaspoons vanilla
Mini marshamallows

In a mixing bowl, mix butter, sugar, eggs, cocoa powder, flour, baking powder, salt, and vanilla. Spread into a cookie sheet (jelly roll pan) with sides. Bake at 350 degrees for no more than 20 minutes until set. Sprinkle mini marshmallows on top and bake just until they are puffed up. Cool.

TOPPING:

1½ cups chocolate chips
1 cup peanut butter

2½ cups crisp rice cereal

In a large saucepan, melt chocolate chips and peanut butter together. Mix in cereal. Spread over marshmallows.

MRS. JOSEPH MILLER, Navarre, OH

Magic Cookie Bars

½ cup margarine or butter
1½ cups graham cracker crumbs
1 (14 ounce) can sweetened
  condensed milk

1 cup chopped nuts
6 ounces chocolate chips
1 cup shredded coconut

Heat oven to 350 degrees. Place margarine in a 9x13-inch pan and melt in oven. Sprinkle cracker crumbs over butter and press evenly. Drizzle condensed milk over crumbs. Sprinkle with nuts, chocolate chips, and coconut. Press down firmly. Bake for 25 to 30 minutes. Cool and cut into bars.

Mrs. Menno J. Miller, Gallipolis, OH

Our Favorite Bars

These bars are soft and loaded with flavor.

1 cup butter
1 cup coconut or vegetable oil
1 cup peanut butter
2½ cups raw sugar
¾ cup sorghum
6 eggs
2 teaspoons vanilla

2 teaspoons baking soda
2 teaspoons baking powder
2 cups whole-wheat flour
2 cups all-purpose flour
4 cups oats
2 cups chocolate chips

In a bowl, beat together butter, oil, peanut butter, sugar, sorghum, eggs, and vanilla. Add baking soda, baking powder, flours, and oats. Mix well. Add chocolate chips, mixing well. Divide into 2 9x13-inch pans. Bake at 350 degrees for 20 minutes until set. Don't overbake.

Norma Yutzy, Drakesville, IA

Chocolate Chip Meringue Bars

We liked when our older sisters made these bars when the cousins got together. One time they accidently put salt in place of white sugar into the batter, and we couldn't understand why we couldn't eat them.

1 cup butter	1 teaspoon baking powder
½ cup sugar	¼ teaspoon baking soda
½ cup brown sugar	¼ teaspoon salt
3 egg yolks	12 ounces chocolate chips
1 teaspoon vanilla	3 egg whites
3 tablespoons water	1 cup brown sugar
2 cups flour	

In a bowl, cream butter, sugar, ½ cup brown sugar, egg yolks, vanilla, and water. In another bowl, sift flour, baking powder, baking soda, and salt. Add to sugar mixture. Mix well. Spread thinly onto an ungreased cookie sheet. Sprinkle with chocolate chips. In a bowl, beat egg whites until foamy, then add 1 cup brown sugar ¼ cup at a time. Beat until stiff. Spread over chips and bake at 350 degrees for 30 minutes or more until lightly brown. Cool and cut into bars.

Mrs. Melvin Schlabach, Dayton, PA

Coconut Meringue Bars

¾ cup butter	1 teaspoon baking powder
1½ cups brown sugar, divided	¼ teaspoon baking soda
½ cup sugar	¼ teaspoon salt
3 eggs, separated	2 cups chocolate chips
1 teaspoon vanilla	1 cup shredded coconut
2 cups flour	

In a mixing bowl, cream butter, ½ cup brown sugar, and sugar. Add egg yolks and vanilla. In another bowl, combine flour, baking powder, baking soda, and salt. Add to creamed mixture. Spread into a 9x13-inch pan. Sprinkle with chocolate chips and coconut. In a clean bowl, beat egg whites until stiff. Add 1 cup brown sugar 1 tablespoon at a time. Spread on top of chocolate chips. Bake at 350 degrees for 25 minutes until golden brown.

Mrs. Freeman (Sylvia) Mast, Constable, NY

CREAM-FILLED DOUGHNUT BARS

These are delicious! When we get together for our family night, the girls often bring one pan of these. So good!

1 cup lukewarm water
1 tablespoon yeast
¼ cup brown sugar
1 egg, beaten

¼ cup oil
1 teaspoon salt
1 cup doughnut mix
3 cups flour

Combine water and yeast; let stand until foamy. Add brown sugar, egg, oil, and salt; mix well. Add doughnut mix; mix well. Add flour 1 cup at a time, kneading well. Cover and let rise 1 hour, then punch down and roll out on a large well-greased cookie sheet and let rise 1 hour. Bake at 350 degrees for 12 to 15 minutes. Cool completely, then cut in half lengthwise.

FILLING:

1 cup milk, scalded
1 (3 ounce) box vanilla
  instant pudding mix

1 (8 ounce) package
  cream cheese
1 (8 ounce) tub whipped topping

Mix filling ingredients together and spread on bottom layer. Put top layer back on. Frost with your favorite caramel frosting and sprinkle with cinnamon and sugar.

LORENE HERSCHBERGER, Sullivan, IL

CARAMEL TOFFEE SQUARES

FIRST LAYER:

½ cup plus 2 tablespoons butter   ¼ cup sugar
1¼ cups flour

Mix butter, flour, and sugar and press into a 9x13-inch pan. Bake at 350 degrees for 10 minutes or until lightly browned.

SECOND LAYER:

1 cup butter   4 tablespoons corn syrup
1 (14 ounce) can condensed milk   1 cup brown sugar

In a saucepan, mix butter, condensed milk, corn syrup, and brown sugar and bring to a boil. Boil for 5 minutes, stirring constantly. Remove from heat and beat well. Spread over crust and cool.

THIRD LAYER:

1½ cups chocolate chips   2 tablespoons oil

Combine chocolate chips with oil and melt, stirring until smooth. Spread over caramel layer.

NANCY S. YODER, Allensville, PA

Butter Pecan Banana Bars

2½ cups flour
1⅔ cups sugar
1¼ teaspoons baking powder
1¼ teaspoons baking soda
Pinch salt

¾ cup shortening
⅔ cup buttermilk or sour milk
1¼ cups mashed ripe bananas
2 eggs
½ cup chopped pecans

In a bowl, mix flour, sugar, baking powder, baking soda, and salt. Add shortening, buttermilk, and bananas, stirring until moistened. Add eggs and beat well. Stir in nuts. Pour in a greased 10x15-inch pan. Bake at 350 degrees for 20 to 25 minutes. Cool and frost with your favorite frosting.

Mrs. Monroe Miller, Blanchard, MI

Peanut Butter Dream Bars

2 cups butter, melted
2 cups brown sugar
2 teaspoons baking soda
½ teaspoon salt
3 cups flour

3 cups oats
1 (14 ounce) can sweetened
  condensed milk
⅓ cup peanut butter
M&Ms

In a bowl, blend butter and brown sugar. Mix in baking soda, salt, flour, and oats. Press into a 10x15-inch jelly roll pan. Bake at 350 degrees for 10 minutes. In a bowl, combine condensed milk and peanut butter. Spread over hot crust. Sprinkle with M&Ms and bake 8 minutes.

Martha Miller, Hillsboro, OH

Peanut Butter Fingers

½ cup sugar
½ cup brown sugar
½ cup butter
⅓ cup peanut butter
1 egg
½ teaspoon vanilla
1 cup flour

½ teaspoon baking soda
¼ teaspoon salt
1 cup oats
Chocolate chips
½ cup powdered sugar
¼ cup peanut butter
Milk

In a mixing bowl, cream sugar, brown sugar, butter, and ⅓ cup peanut butter. Add egg and vanilla; mix. Add flour, baking soda, salt, and oats, mixing well. Spread into a greased 9x13-inch pan. Bake at 350 degrees for 15 to 20 minutes. While still hot, sprinkle with chocolate chips. Let stand 5 minutes, then spread chocolate to cover base. Cool. Combine powdered sugar, ¼ cup peanut butter, and enough milk to create a mixture you can drizzle over the chocolate.

Mrs. Menno J. Miller, Gallipolis, OH

Frosted Pumpkin Bars

1¼ cups sugar
½ cup oil
4 eggs, beaten
2 cups flour
½ teaspoon salt

2 teaspoons cinnamon
1 teaspoon baking soda
1 teaspoon baking powder
1 cup pumpkin puree
1 cup chopped nuts

In a mixing bowl, combine all ingredients until well mixed. Pour into a greased 12x17-inch pan. Bake at 350 degrees for 20 minutes or until it tests done.

Cream Cheese Icing:

4 ounces cream cheese, softened
6 tablespoons butter, softened
3½ cups powdered sugar

1 tablespoon milk
1 teaspoon vanilla

In a mixing bowl, combine all ingredients until smooth. Spread over cooled bars.

Mrs. Joseph Miller, Navarre, OH

PUMPKIN BARS

4 eggs
1⅔ cups sugar
1 cup oil
2 cups pumpkin puree
2 cups flour

2 teaspoons cinnamon
2 teaspoons baking powder
1 teaspoon baking soda
1 teaspoon salt

In a mixing bowl, beat eggs, sugar, oil, and pumpkin. Add flour, cinnamon, baking powder, baking soda, and salt. Mix well. Pour into an ungreased 10x15-inch jelly roll pan. Bake at 350 degrees for 30 minutes. Cool. Frost with cream cheese frosting.

MENNO J. YODERS, Berlin, PA

COOKIE STICKS

A quick cookie just the right shape for dunking into milk.

1 cup oil
1 cup sugar
1 cup brown sugar
2 eggs
2 teaspoons vanilla

3 cups flour
1 teaspoon baking soda
1 teaspoon salt
2 cups chocolate chips

In a mixing bowl, combine oil, sugar, brown sugar, eggs, and vanilla; mix well. Sift together flour, baking soda, and salt; add to creamed mixture. Divide dough into 4 pieces. On 2 greased baking sheets, shape each portion into a 5x15-inch rectangle set about 3 inches apart. Sprinkle each portion of dough with chocolate chips and lightly press them in. Bake at 350 degrees for 6 to 7 minutes. Cool for 5 minutes. Cut into 1-inch strips.

IOANA PETERSHEIM, Fredericktown, OH

Giant Chocolate Chip Cookie

1 cup butter, melted
1 cup brown sugar
½ cup sugar
2 eggs
1 (3 ounce) box vanilla
    instant pudding mix

1½ teaspoons vanilla
½ teaspoon salt
1 teaspoon baking soda
2 cups flour
2 cups Hershey's Kisses

In a mixing bowl, cream butter, brown sugar, and sugar. Beat in eggs. Add pudding mix and vanilla. Mix in salt, baking soda, and flour. Fold in candy. Spread into a 15-inch cast-iron skillet. Bake at 350 degrees for 15 to 18 minutes. Do not overbake.

BRENDA GRABER, Hamptonville, NC

Chocolate Chip Pudding Cookies

A family favorite.

2 cups brown sugar
1 small box vanilla instant
    pudding mix
1 cup butter, softened
3 eggs

1½ teaspoons vanilla
1 teaspoon baking soda
3½ cups flour
2 cups chocolate chips

In a mixing bowl, combine brown sugar and pudding mix. Add butter, eggs, and vanilla, stirring well. Combine baking soda with flour and mix into first mixture. Mix well. Stir in chocolate chips. Drop onto ungreased baking sheets and bake at 350 degrees for 8 to 10 minutes. Don't overbake. Let them sit a few minutes on baking sheets before removing. We have at times frosted these.

MRS. JOSEPH MILLER, Navarre, OH

Blue Bonnet Chocolate Chip Cookies

My comfort foods are often sweets. There is nothing like warm chocolate chip cookies just out of the oven. Delicious!

¾ cup butter, melted and cooled
1½ cups brown sugar
1 egg
2 cups flour

1 teaspoon baking soda
½ teaspoon salt
2 teaspoons vanilla
1 cup chocolate chips

In a mixing bowl, cream butter and brown sugar. Add egg. Mix well. Add flour, baking soda, and salt. Add vanilla and chocolate chips. Mix well. Bake at 350 degrees for 8 to 10 minutes. Don't overbake. They are best if you take them out when they look like they are not quite done.

Ida Byler, Frazeysburg, OH

No-Bake Fudge Cookies

These are one of my favorites to eat on a lazy Sunday afternoon with freshly popped popcorn. Mom loves them warm, and they always remind me of her.

1 cup sugar
1 cup brown sugar
½ cup butter
½ cup milk
½ teaspoon salt

1 cup chocolate chips (or more)
½ to ¾ cup peanut butter
½ cup shredded coconut
  (optional)
2 to 4 cups quick oats

In a saucepan, bring sugar, brown sugar, butter, milk, and salt to a boil for 3 to 5 minutes. Remove from heat and add chocolate chips and peanut butter. Stir until melted. Add coconut and oats to desired consistency. Drop by tablespoonful onto waxed paper-lined cookie sheets. Eat warm or refrigerate.

Ida Byler, Frazeysburg, OH

Espresso Cookies

1 cup butter, softened
6 tablespoons sugar
2 cups brown sugar
2 large eggs
4 teaspoons vanilla

3½ cups flour
1 teaspoon baking powder
1 teaspoon baking soda
1 tablespoon instant coffee
2 cups chocolate chips

Cream together butter, sugar, and brown sugar. Add eggs and vanilla. Add flour, baking powder, baking soda, and coffee. Mix in chocolate chips. Bake at 375 degrees for 10 to 12 minutes. Don't overbake.

MALACHI AND IDA MAE STAUFFER, Homer City, PA

Chai Sugar Cookies

1 egg
1 egg yolk
2 tablespoons honey
1 cup sugar
10 tablespoons butter, softened
½ teaspoon ground cloves
½ teaspoon allspice
1 teaspoon ginger

1 teaspoon cardamom or
  pumpkin pie spice
2 teaspoons cinnamon
½ teaspoon salt
1 teaspoon cornstarch
2 cups plus 2 tablespoons flour
2 teaspoons baking powder

In a mixing bowl, blend egg, egg yolk, honey, sugar, and butter. Add cloves, allspice, ginger, cardamom, cinnamon, salt, and cornstarch. Mix in flour and baking powder. Roll dough into balls. Flatten with a spatula into a baking sheet. Bake at 350 degrees for 12 to 14 minutes. Cool. Drizzle with espresso glaze.

ESPRESSO GLAZE:

1¼ cups powdered sugar

2 tablespoons strong coffee

Blend sugar and coffee together until smooth.

MARLENE STOLTZFUS, Gap, PA

Café Cookies

1 cup sugar
1 cup brown sugar
1 cup butter
2 eggs
2 tablespoons instant coffee

3 cups flour
2 teaspoons baking soda
1 teaspoon salt
1 bag chocolate chips (optional)
1 cup chopped nuts (optional)

In a mixing bowl, cream sugar, brown sugar, and butter. Mix in eggs and instant coffee. Add flour, baking soda, and salt. If using, mix in chocolate chips and/or nuts. Drop by spoonful or cookie scoop onto baking sheets. Bake at 350 degrees for 12 minutes.

Mrs. Mary Mast, Danville, OH

Brown Sugar Cookies

My grandma used to make these. We all liked them,
and even sometimes sneaked an extra one.

9 eggs
9 cups brown sugar
3 cups oil
3 teaspoons vanilla

14½ cups flour
1 tablespoon baking soda
1½ teaspoons salt
3 cups buttermilk

In a large mixing bowl, beat eggs. Add brown sugar, oil, and vanilla. Sift together flour, baking soda, and salt. Add alternately with buttermilk. You can refrigerate the dough overnight if desired. Drop spoonfuls of dough on ungreased baking sheets. Bake at 350 degrees for 10 minutes. Yields 9 dozen.

Frosting:

1 cup butter
2 cups milk

4 cups brown sugar
8 cups powdered sugar, sifted

In a large saucepan over medium heat, melt butter. Add milk and brown sugar, stirring to dissolve sugar. Bring mixture to a boil and boil for 2 minutes. Remove from heat and add powdered sugar, stirring quickly until smooth. Working quickly before frosting hardens, spread about 1 tablespoon frosting onto each cookie.

David Byler, New Castle, PA

Soft Sugar Cookies

*I loved when we came to Grandmother's
house and she had these cookies on hand.*

3 cups lard
3 cups sugar
3 cups brown sugar
5 eggs
3 cups sour milk or buttermilk

3 teaspoons lemon extract
9 cups flour
6 teaspoons baking powder
3 teaspoons baking soda

In a large mixing bowl, cream lard, sugar, and brown sugar. Mix in eggs.
Add milk and lemon extract. In a separate bowl, mix flour, baking powder,
and baking soda. Slowly add dry mixture to wet mixture until well combined. Drop dough by spoonfuls on ungreased baking sheets. Bake at 350
degrees for 10 to 12 minutes. Do not overbake.

VERNA D. GINGERICH, Mount Ayr, IA

Spicy Sugar Cookies

1½ cups shortening
2 cups sugar
2 eggs
½ cup honey
4 tablespoons milk
2 teaspoons vanilla
5 cups flour

3 teaspoons baking soda
1½ teaspoons salt
1½ teaspoons nutmeg
2 teaspoons cinnamon
Milk
Sugar

In a mixing bowl, cream shortening and sugar. Add eggs, then honey, milk,
and vanilla. In another bowl, combine flour, baking soda, salt, nutmeg, and
cinnamon. Add to wet mixture. Form dough into balls; dip into some milk
then into sugar. Place on baking sheets and bake at 350 degrees for 10
minutes.

ESTHER L. MILLER, Fredericktown, OH

Maryann Raber Cookies

We make these quite often.

2 cups sugar
2 cups brown sugar
1½ cups butter
½ cup butter, browned
4 eggs
1 teaspoon vanilla

2 cups milk
Pinch salt
5 teaspoons baking powder
3 teaspoons baking soda
    dissolved in a little vinegar
7 cups flour

In a large mixing bowl, cream sugar, brown sugar, butter, and browned butter. Add eggs and vanilla. Add milk. Mix well. Add salt, baking powder, baking soda with vinegar, and flour. Mix well. Refrigerate overnight. Bake at 350 degrees for 8 to 10 minutes.

Mrs. Melvin Schlabach, Dayton, PA

Frosted Cream Cookies

2 cups sugar
2 cups melted butter
  or margarine
6 egg yolks
2 cups molasses

1 cup water
2 tablespoons baking soda
1 tablespoon cinnamon
2 teaspoons baking powder
10 cups flour

In a large bowl, cream sugar with butter. Mix in egg yolks and molasses. Add water. In another bowl, sift baking soda, cinnamon, baking powder, and flour. Add to creamed mixture. Cover and refrigerate overnight. Roll out dough ¼ to ½ inch thick and cut as desired. Bake at 375 degrees for 8 to 10 minutes. Cool.

FROSTING:

3 cups sugar
8 tablespoons water

6 egg whites, beaten

In a saucepan, bring sugar and water to about halfway between soft and hard ball stage. Pour over beaten egg whites. Beat until stiff. Spread onto cookies.

MALINDA GINGERICH, Spartansburg, PA

Monster Cookies

¼ cup butter, softened	2½ teaspoons baking soda
¾ cup sugar	¼ cup flour
1 cup brown sugar	4½ cups oats
4 eggs	½ pound M&Ms
1 pound peanut butter	8 ounces chocolate chips

Mix all together to make a stiff dough. Drop by spoonful or cookie scoop onto ungreased cookie sheets. Bake at 350 degrees for 10 minutes. Do not overbake.

Mrs. Joseph Miller, Navarre, OH

Simple Peanut Butter Cookies

This is a handy recipe when you are short on eggs.

1 cup butter or lard	¼ teaspoon salt
2 cups sucanat or light brown sugar	1½ teaspoons baking soda dissolved in 3 tablespoons hot water
1 cup peanut butter	
3 cups flour	

In a mixing bowl, cream butter, sugar, and peanut butter. Add flour, salt, and baking soda mixture. Mix well. Form balls, roll in some sugar, and flatten onto a baking sheet. Bake at 350 degrees for 10 to 12 minutes. Leave on cookie sheet for about 5 minutes to cool.

Mrs. Mary Mast, Danville, OH

PEANUT BUTTER MELT-AWAY COOKIES

1 cup peanut butter
1 cup sugar
1 egg
½ teaspoon vanilla

1 teaspoon baking soda
1½ cups flour
1 cup chocolate chips

In a mixing bowl, cream peanut butter and sugar. Add egg, vanilla, and baking soda. Stir in flour. Add chocolate chips. Roll dough into balls and place on baking sheets. Bake at 350 degrees for 10 to 15 minutes. Makes 2 dozen.

NANCY S. YODER, Allensville, PA

Molasses Cookies

2 cups sugar
1 cup shortening
2 eggs
½ cup sorghum or molasses
1 teaspoon vanilla
4½ cups flour

2¼ teaspoons nutmeg
1 teaspoon baking soda
½ teaspoon salt
½ teaspoon ginger
½ teaspoon cinnamon

In a bowl, cream sugar and shortening. Add eggs, sorghum, and vanilla, mixing well. In another bowl, sift together flour, nutmeg, baking soda, salt, ginger, and cinnamon. Add to creamed mixture and form dough into a log. Wrap in plastic wrap and chill at least 2 hours or overnight. Slice about ¼ inch thick and bake on ungreased cookie sheets at 350 degrees for approximately 10 minutes until just browning on edges. Let cool awhile on pans before moving to wire racks.

Note: You can adjust the spice to your taste. We like 1 teaspoon cinnamon with no nutmeg or ginger.

These cookies can be made and kept for about 2 months, so they are great to make ahead of a busy season. If kept in a container that is not completely airtight, they will become chewy, which we like best. You can even put them in a pillowcase and hang it from basement rafters. But ours almost never lasted long unless our mother hid them.

Mrs. Moses Swartz, Mount Ayr, IA

MOLASSES COFFEE COOKIES

A family favorite. Good to dip in hot chocolate.

2 cups lard
3 cups brown sugar
2 cups molasses
2 cups hot coffee
6 teaspoons baking soda

2 eggs, beaten
6 teaspoons vanilla
1 teaspoon salt
10 to 12 cups flour
(approximately)

In a large mixing bowl, cream lard and brown sugar. Mix in molasses, hot coffee, and baking soda. When mixture has cooled some, add eggs, vanilla, and salt. Slowly work in flour until it makes a soft dough. Drop dough by spoonful onto ungreased baking sheets. Bake at 350 degrees for 10 minutes.

VERNA D. GINGERICH, Mount Ayr, IA

WHOOPIE PIES

1 cup shortening
2 cups sugar
2 eggs, beaten
1 teaspoon vanilla
4 cups flour

1 cup cocoa powder
1 teaspoon salt
1 cup sour milk
3 teaspoons baking soda
1 cup hot water

In a mixing bowl, cream together shortening, sugar, eggs, and vanilla. In a separate bowl, sift together flour, cocoa powder, and salt. Add dry mixture to wet mixture alternately with sour milk. Add baking soda to water and stir into batter. Drop by spoonful onto cookie sheets and bake at 350 degrees for 7 to 10 minutes.

Note: Sour milk can be made by adding 2 tablespoons vinegar to 1 scant cup milk.

CREAM CHEESE ICING:

4 ounces cream cheese, softened
2 cups powdered sugar

¼ cup butter, softened
1 cup marshmallow crème

Mix cream cheese and powdered sugar. Add butter and mix well. Blend in marshmallow crème. Spread icing between flat sides of 2 cookies and sandwich together.

DELILA SWARTZENTRUBER, West Salem, OH

CHOCOLATE CHIP WHOOPIE PIES

2 cups sugar
1 cup oil
2 eggs
2 teaspoons baking powder
1 teaspoon baking soda
¾ teaspoon salt

2 tablespoons vanilla
½ cup water
4 cups bread flour
1½ cups sour cream
2 cups mini chocolate chips

In a mixing bowl, blend sugar and oil. Add eggs and mix well. Add baking powder, baking soda, salt, and vanilla. Mix well. Add water and flour, then fold in sour cream. Stir in chocolate chips. Drop by spoonful onto cookie sheets and bake at 375 degrees for 8 minutes. When cool, place your favorite frosting between 2 cookies.

ELI AND ELSIE MILLER, Thurman, OH

MOCHA SANDWICH COOKIES

2 cups brown sugar
1 cup oil
½ cup sour cream
2 eggs
2 teaspoons vanilla
5 teaspoons instant coffee
   dissolved in ¼ cup hot water
3 cups flour

¾ cup cocoa powder
2 teaspoons baking soda
¼ teaspoon salt
¼ teaspoon pepper
Powdered sugar
Vanilla ice cream or
   cream cheese filling

In a mixing bowl, blend brown sugar, oil, sour cream, eggs, vanilla, and coffee; mix well. Add flour, cocoa powder, baking soda, salt, and pepper. Mix well and chill. Roll dough into balls and dip into powdered sugar. Press down a little onto baking sheets. Bake at 350 degrees for 8 minutes. Don't overbake. When cookies are completely cooled, spread slightly thawed ice cream between 2 cookies, wrap each sandwich in plastic wrap, and freeze. Or, spread cookies with cream cheese filling.

CREAM CHEESE FILLING:

1 (8 ounce) package cream
   cheese, softened
1 stick butter, softened

2 teaspoons instant coffee
   dissolved in ¼ cup hot
   water and cooled
6 cups powdered sugar
   (approximately)

In a bowl, blend cream cheese and butter. Add coffee and mix well. Add enough powdered sugar to make a thick spread.

MRS. DAVID RABER, Millersburg, OH

CARAMEL CANDY

This is one of our favorite candies we make for Christmas.

1 pound brown sugar
1 cup corn syrup
1 teaspoon cream of tartar

1 (14 ounce) can sweetened condensed milk
½ pound butter
1 teaspoon vanilla

In a saucepan, mix brown sugar, corn syrup, cream of tartar, condensed milk, and butter. Cook to 240 degrees on a candy thermometer, stirring constantly. Remove from heat and add vanilla. Pour into a greased cake pan. When cooled, cut into squares and dip each into melted chocolate or wrap with waxed paper.

Tips: I use heavy cream instead of sweetened condensed milk. Either should work. If you want a stiffer caramel, cook it to 245 degrees.

Mrs. Joseph Miller, Navarre, OH

SCOTCHAROOS

1 cup corn syrup
1 cup sugar
1 cup peanut butter
6 cups crisp rice cereal

½ (12 ounce) bag vanilla coating wafers
½ (11 ounce) bag butterscotch chips

In a saucepan, melt together corn syrup, sugar, and peanut butter. In a large bowl, place cereal. Pour melted sauce over cereal and mix well to coat. Press into a jelly roll pan. In another saucepan, melt together vanilla coating wafers and butterscotch chips. Spread over cereal. Cut into bars.

David Byler, New Castle, PA

Grandpa's Fudge

½ cup butter
4½ cups sugar
1 can evaporated milk
1 cup marshmallow crème
1 (13 ounce) bar sweetened
   chocolate, grated

2 (12 ounce) packages
   chocolate chips
2 teaspoons vanilla
2 cups walnuts, coarsely
   chopped

Combine butter, sugar, and milk. Cook for 5½ minutes, stirring constantly. Remove from heat. Add marshmallow crème, grated chocolate, chocolate chips, and vanilla. Beat until well mixed then add nuts. Beat until well mixed and smooth. Pour into a buttered 9x13-inch pan. Cool until firm then cut. Yield: 5 pounds.

Rachel Schlabach, Millersburg, OH

STRAWBERRY FUDGE

This is Grandma's recipe that she used to make every Christmas.

3 cups sugar
4 tablespoons strawberry gelatin
⅛ teaspoon salt
¾ cup milk
½ cup heavy cream

1 teaspoon white corn syrup
2 tablespoons butter
1 teaspoon vanilla
¼ cup chopped walnuts (optional)

In a buttered 3-quart saucepan, combine sugar, gelatin, salt, milk, cream, and corn syrup. Bring mixture to a boil over moderate heat, stirring constantly. Then cook without stirring until candy reaches 230 degrees or soft ball stage when dropped in water. Remove from heat and add butter and vanilla but DO NOT STIR. Cool without stirring until outside of pan becomes lukewarm. Stir in nuts and beat until candy loses its glossy shine. Pour into a 9x9-inch pan or mini cupcake pans lined with cupcake paper liners.

MALINDA GINGERICH, Spartansburg, PA

CHOCOLATE MINT PATTIES

A Christmas favorite.

1 (8 ounce) package
    cream cheese
½ cup butter

2 pounds powdered sugar
Peppermint oil to taste

Mix all ingredients together. Use more or less powdered sugar, just enough to easily handle the mixture. Form into tiny patties or logs that you can slice. Chill.

CHOCOLATE COATING:

3 cups semisweet
    chocolate chips

3 tablespoons shortening

In a double boiler, heat chocolate and shortening, stirring to combine. Dip mint patties in chocolate. Place on waxed paper to dry.

MRS. JOSEPH MILLER, Navarre, OH

Easter Eggs

Grandma used to make these for Easter, and now my mom does every year to give to grandchildren. They are really sweet but delicious! One of Dad's favorites. We have also made them for Christmas.

2 pounds powdered sugar
1 (14 ounce) can sweetened
  condensed milk
1 cup butter, softened

2 cups chopped nuts
Shredded coconut
½ teaspoon maple flavoring
Milk chocolate for coating

In a bowl, mix powdered sugar, condensed milk, butter, nuts, coconut in preferred amount, and maple flavoring. Refrigerate until firm enough to form into egg shapes. Place on waxed paper-lined cookie sheets. Refrigerate until firm. Melt chocolate and dip eggs in 1 at a time. Allow to fully dry.

IDA BYLER, Frazeysburg, OH

Oven Caramel Corn

2 cups dark brown sugar
2 sticks butter
¼ cup sorghum molasses
1 teaspoon salt

1 teaspoon baking soda
1 tablespoon vanilla
6 quarts popped corn

In a saucepan, combine brown sugar, butter, and molasses and bring to a boil for 5 minutes. Remove from heat and add salt, baking soda, and vanilla. Pour over corn. Spread in a baking pan and bake at 200 degrees for 1 hour, stirring every 15 minutes. Cool and store in airtight container.

ELLA ARLENE YODER, Arcola, IL

Vanilla Ice Cream

¾ cup evaporated cane sugar
2 tablespoons cornstarch
½ teaspoon salt
8 cups milk, divided
4 egg yolks
4 egg whites, beaten

¾ cup brown sugar
2 teaspoons vanilla
¼ teaspoon maple flavoring
1 cup heavy cream or
  evaporated milk

Mix cane sugar, cornstarch, salt, and 4 cups milk in a saucepan. Beat in egg yolks and cook until thickened. Remove from heat. Add beaten egg whites, brown sugar, vanilla, and maple flavoring. Cool completely. Add cream and 4 cups milk. Place in a 1-gallon ice cream freezer and freeze according to freezer directions.

Mrs. Joseph Miller, Navarre, OH

CHOCOLATE ICE CREAM

½ cup evaporated cane sugar
2 tablespoons cornstarch
½ teaspoon salt
8 cups milk, divided
4 egg yolks
4 egg whites, beaten

¾ cup brown sugar
2 teaspoons vanilla
1 cup heavy cream or
  evaporated milk
1 cup chocolate milk powder

Mix cane sugar, cornstarch, salt, and 4 cups milk in a saucepan. Beat in egg yolks and cook until thickened. Remove from heat. Add beaten egg whites, brown sugar, and vanilla. Cool completely. Add cream, 4 cups milk, and chocolate milk powder. Place in a 1-gallon ice cream freezer and freeze according to freezer directions.

MRS. JOSEPH MILLER, Navarre, OH

Chocolate Dip

1½ cups sugar
3 tablespoons butter
4 tablespoons cocoa powder

1 cup evaporated milk
1 teaspoon vanilla

In a saucepan, boil together sugar, butter, cocoa powder, and milk for 7 minutes. Add vanilla. Serve warm over ice cream.

Lydiann Yoder, Andover, OH

Party Mix

A favorite sweet and salty staple at our house over the holidays, especially as a bedtime snack.

5 to 6 boxes cereal or snacks
    (Froot Loops, Honeycomb,
    Cheerios, pretzels, etc.)
2 cups butter
1 tablespoon seasoned salt

1 tablespoon onion salt
    or garlic powder
2 tablespoons
    Worcestershire sauce

Place cereal and snacks in a large roasting pan. In a saucepan, melt together butter, seasoned salt, onion salt, and Worcestershire sauce. Pour over cereal and mix well to coat. Bake at 200 degrees for 1 hour, stirring every 15 minutes.

Nelson and Joann Miller Family, Fredericktown, OH

*In the multitude
of my anxieties within
me, Your comforts
delight my soul.*

PSALM 94:19

Index of Contributors

INDEX OF RECIPES BY SECTION

INDEX OF RECIPES BY KEY INGREDIENTS

OTHER COOKBOOKS FROM WANDA E. BRUNSTETTER

Wanda E. Brunstetter's Amish Friends Cookbook: Volume 1

Wanda E. Brunstetter's Amish Friends Cookbook: Volume 2

The Best of Amish Friends Cookbook Collection

Wanda E. Brunstetter's Amish Friends Cookbook: Desserts

Wanda E. Brunstetter's Amish Friends Christmas Cookbook

Wanda E. Brunstetter's Amish Friends Harvest Cookbook

Amish Cooking Class Cookbook

Wanda E. Brunstetter's Amish Friends Gatherings Cookbook

Wanda E. Brunstetter's Amish Friends Christmas Cookbook

Wanda E. Brunstetter's Amish Friends Farmhouse Favorites Cookbook

Wanda E. Brunstetter's Amish Friends from Scratch Cookbook

Wanda E. Brunstetter's Amish Friends Healthy Options Cookbook

Wanda E. Brunstetter's Amish Friends Baking Cookbook

Wanda E. Brunstetter's Amish Friends 4 Seasons Cookbook

Wanda E. Brunstetter's Amish Friends No Waste Cookbook

Wanda E. Brunstetter's Amish Friends One-Pan Wonders Cookbook

Wanda E. Brunstetter's Amish Friends Life Hacks

Wanda E. Brunstetter's Amish Friends Outdoor Cookbook

Available Wherever Books Are Sold
or at www.barbourbooks.com

BARBOUR
PUBLISHING